Organic Food Marketing
in Urban Centres of India

Nina Osswald
Manoj Kumar Menon

ICCOA
International Competence Centre for Organic Agriculture

Nina Osswald and Manoj Kumar Menon (2013): Organic Food Marketing in Urban Centres of India. Bangalore: ICCOA.

Research funded by
Federal Ministry of Education and Research (BMBF), Germany, as part of the programme "Research for the Sustainable Development of the Megacities of Tomorrow - Energy and Climate efficient Structures in Urban Growth Centres", and supported by ICCOA

Research directed by
Nina Osswald, Research Associate at Humboldt University Berlin, Department of Agricultural Economics and Social Sciences, as part of the project "Hyderabad as a Megacity of Tomorrow" (www.sustainable-hyderabad.de)

First published in March 2013
ISBN 978-81-925226-3-0 (International Print Edition)

Cover designed by
Vivek S., Abhinav Gupta

Published by
International Competence Centre for Organic Agriculture (ICCOA)
951 C, 15th Cross, 8th Main, Ideal Homes Township,
Rajarajeshwarinagar, Bangalore - 560 098, Karnataka, India
Tel: +91 (0)80 2860 1183, Fax: +91 (0)80 2860 0935
Email: info@iccoa.org
Web: www.iccoa.org

Contents

Foreword   iii

About This Book   ix

About the Authors   xi

Acknowledgements   xii

Tables, Figures and Case Studies   v

Glossary and List of Acronyms   vii

1   Introduction   1

   1.1   Context: The Booming Indian Organic Market?   1

   1.2   Objectives of the Study   4

2   Analytical Approach and Methodology   7

   2.1   Scope of the Study   7

   2.2   Study Design and Research Methodology   8

   2.3   Limitations and Need for Further Research   9

3   The Organic Sector in India   11

   3.1   Sustainable Agriculture: Definitions   11

   3.2   Organic Production and Domestic Market Size   16

   3.3   Institutional Context and Regulations   22

4   Organic Food Distribution Systems   29

   4.1   Domestic Market Structures and Classification Framework   29

   4.2   Overview: Organic Retail in Mumbai, Bangalore and Hyderabad   36

   4.3   Organic Specialty Stores, Markets and Health Food Stores   39

   4.4   Direct Marketing and Community-Supported Agriculture   48

   4.5   Restaurants and Catering   60

4.6	Online Retail and Home Delivery Services	61
4.7	General Trade and Organized Retail	63
5	**Challenges and Success Stories in Organic Marketing**	**67**
5.1	Product Availability and Working with Suppliers	67
5.2	Organizational Models and Legal Context	72
5.3	Building Efficient Supply Chains and Retail Channels	79
5.4	Sustainability along the Supply Chain	86
5.5	Certification: Opportunity or Obstacle?	89
5.6	Building Awareness and Meeting Consumer Needs	93
6	**Conclusion**	**103**
6.1	Summary of Findings	103
6.2	Recommendations	108
Appendix 1: Certification agencies accredited under NPOP		*115*
Appendix 2: Organic stakeholders by distribution channel and city		*120*
References		*123*

Tables, Figures and Case Studies

List of Tables

Table 2-1: Sample size of outlet surveys and interviews with organic stakeholders   9

Table 3-1: Organic production and marketing data overview   19

Table 4-1: Ownership and support structures in the organic production sector   34

Table 4-2: Organic market coverage in terms of stakeholders and outlets per city   37

Table 4-3: Bangalore: Estimated sales per distribution channel and total market size projection   38

Table 4-4: Organic stores per city by opening year   40

Table 4-5: Ownership and support structures in organic retail   44

Table 5-1: Empirical studies on consumer perceptions and willingness to pay   98

List of Figures

Figure 2-1: Overview map of the three cities covered by this study   8

Figure 3-1: Growth of export and domestic market shares since 2005   20

Figure 3-2: Official India Organic label for products certified according to NSOP (National Standards for Organic Production)   23

Figure 3-3: PGS (Participatory Guarantee System) Organic label awarded by the PGS Organic India Council   24

Figure 3-4: PGS-India labels for in-conversion and fully organic products developed by NCOF   25

Figure 4-1: Classification criteria for stakeholders in the organic food sector   30

Figure 4-2: Organic retail models in urban centres   32

Figure 5-1: Label developed by ICCOA for marketing organically grown vegetables from farmers in Karnataka   82

List of Case Studies

Case Study 1:   24 Mantra: Sresta Bioproducts Pvt. Ltd.   40
Case Study 2:   Fabindia Pvt. Ltd.   45
Case Study 3:   "No Bargaining": The Farmers' Market in Mumbai   50
Case Study 4:   „Organic Veggies in my Inbox": GORUS in Pune   57
Case Study 5:   Farmer-Owned Success Story: Timbaktu Organic   74
Case Study 6:   Sahaja Aharam Organic Consumer and Producer
                Cooperative   77
Case Study 7:   A Regional Label for Organically Grown Vegetables by
                ICCOA   82
Case Study 8:   "Greens in a Box": MOFCA's Hari Bhari Tokri   100

Glossary and List of Acronyms

AP	Andhra Pradesh
APEDA	Agricultural & Processed Food Products Export Development Authority
APMC	Agricultural Produce Marketing Committee
APGMC	Agricultural Produce Grading, Marking and Certification Act
ASHA	Alliance for Sustainable and Holistic Agriculture
ASSOCHAM	Associated Chambers of Commerce and Industry of India
CROPS	Centre for Rural Operation Programmes Society
CSA	Centre for Sustainable Agriculture (Hyderabad), or Community-Supported Agriculture (to avoid confusion, the acronym is not used only for Community-Supported Agriculture throughout this publication)
CWS	Centre for World Solidarity
DDS	Deccan Development Society
DRDA-IKP	District Rural Development Agency, Ranga Reddy District, a Government Agency for Rural Development, in charge of the state-wide rural poverty reduction project "Indira Kranthi Patham" which is implemented by SERP
FPO	Farmer producer organization
FPO	Fruit Products Order
FSSAI	Food Safety and Standards Authority of India
GHG	Greenhouse gases
GMOs	Genetically modified organisms
HACA	Hyderabad Agricultural Cooperative Association
ICCOA	International Competence Centre for Organic Agriculture
ICS	Internal control system

IFOAM	International Federation of Organic Agriculture Movements
INR	Indian Rupees
INM	Integrated Nutrient Management
IPDM	Integrated Pest and Disease Management
ISCOP	Indian Society for Certification of Organic Production
IWM	Integrated Weed Management
jaggery	Traditional unrefined non-centrifugal sugar made from cane juice
KA	Karnataka
kirana store	Small neighbourhood stores that sell groceries and other daily needs, approximately equivalent to "mom-and-pop stores" in the US
MACCS	Mutually-Aided Consumer Cooperative Society
MH	Maharashtra
NCOF	National Centre of Organic Farming, Department of Agriculture and Cooperation, Ministry of Agriculture, Government of India
NPM	Non-pesticide management, a method of sustainable agriculture that eliminates the use of synthetic pesticides
NSSO	National Sample Survey Office
OFAI	Organic Farming Association of India
PGS	Participatory Guarantee System
RKVY	Rashtriya Krishi Vikas Yojana (National Agriculture Development Plan), a government programme for agricultural development
Sahaja Aharam	"Natural Food" in Telugu; farmer-owned organic brand developed by Centre for Sustainable Agriculture (Hyderabad) and short name for the Sahaja Aharam Mutually Aided Cooperative Federation
SERP	Society for Elimination of Rural Poverty
SHG	Self-help group

About This Book

This study was undertaken as a collaborative effort between the International Competence Centre for Organic Agriculture (ICCOA) in Bangalore and the Humboldt University Berlin, Germany, as part of the project "Hyderabad as a Megacity of Tomorrow: Climate and Energy in a Complex Transition towards Sustainable Hyderabad – Mitigation and Adaptation Strategies by Changing Institutions, Governance Structures, Lifestyles and Consumption Patterns", or Sustainable Hyderabad Project.

ICCOA was founded as a knowledge and learning centre for organic agriculture in India. It is a non-profit organization registered under the Karnataka Societies Registration Act. ICCOA's mission is to serve all stakeholders of organic agriculture in the South Asian region, helping them build their competence and thereby contribute to building organic agriculture practices and businesses that are ecologically, economically and socially sustainable. Its activities comprise advocating organic agriculture; collecting, documenting and disseminating knowledge and information; training and capacity building for individuals and institutions; networking of stakeholders in the organic sector; and providing consultancy services. ICCOA puts great emphasis on facilitating market linkages between producers, processors, retailers and consumers of organic products, and on developing domestic markets in India.

To date, very few studies have been published on the Indian domestic market for organic food. Stakeholders working in the organic sector need more in-depth information about the structure of supply chains and urban markets in order to make organic food available to more people and access the large potential of urban markets.

The present study gives an insight into the current market scenario in urban India, availability of organic products and market structures. It aims to categorize the broad variety of different models of organic food distribution and marketing that exist at present; to identify obstacles to market growth; and to determine the conditions for successful and sustainable market development. This study analyzes the dynamic developments taking place in urban markets and the challenges various stakeholders face in bringing organic food to consumers. It documents emerging strategies and best-practice examples that could help in addressing these challenges, examines how organic supply chains can be organized sustainably, and how the growth of the organic sector can benefit producers, especially small and marginal farmers. Data for this study was gathered during 2011 in a comprehensive survey of the markets for organic food in Mumbai, Bangalore and Hyderabad.

While during the 1990s and early 2000s, the bulk of certified organic produce was exported, the domestic market for organic food has since started to develop dynamically. With more and more shops opening, organic food products have become more readily available in urban centres of India over the past few years. While some grassroots marketing initiatives have a long-standing history, innovative approaches ranging from organic online shopping to community-supported agriculture emerged more recently. Domestic organic sales are expanding mainly because of the growth of the urban middle classes and an increase in health consciousness. Nevertheless, due to a number of obstacles, large segments of the population do not have access to organic food yet.

The major challenges that stakeholders in the domestic market face include lack of a wide product range and consistent product availability, especially for fresh produce; quality control and difficulties in working with scattered producers; lack of institutional support and market linkages for small and marginal producers; supply chain constraints such as inadequate transport infrastructure, storage and cooling facilities; lack of awareness of organic food among consumers; and meeting consumer needs. Case studies from different cities and contexts are used throughout the book to illustrate these points.

Examples of successful organic marketing initiatives already exist across the country, and they need to be shared more widely among the various stakeholders. Part of ICCOA's mission as a knowledge and learning centre for organic agriculture and agribusiness is to facilitate this exchange by disseminating experiences, lessons learned and best practice examples in organic marketing. This information will allow stakeholders on the grassroots level to benefit from the increasing demand for organic food in urban markets and to develop their own marketing initiatives in a sustainable manner. This study is a useful resource for organic manufacturers, for traders, policy makers and researchers. It also includes the most comprehensive bibliography currently available on the Indian domestic market for organic food.

About the Authors

Nina Osswald has a background in Development Geography, with an M.A. degree from the University of Freiburg, Germany. In the past, she worked in different organisations in the sustainable consumption and production sector, and since 2009 has been researching the Indian market for organic food. Nina previously co-authored a publication on *Sustainable Food Consumption and Urban Lifestyles: The Case of Hyderabad, India*. She coordinated the present study on urban market structures as a Research Associate at the Humboldt University Berlin in the Indo-German cooperation project Sustainable Hyderabad.

Manoj Kumar Menon holds a degree in Agricultural Sciences and did his Post-graduation in Management (MBA from FMS, University of Delhi). He has been the Executive Director of ICCOA since 2006. He has worked in the organic agriculture sector in many parts of India, and actively participates and advises policy formulation in some state governments. He was also a co-author of the previous research study *The Market for Organic Foods in India: Consumer Perceptions and Market Potential*, published by ICCOA in 2006.

Acknowledgements

We gratefully acknowledge the support from the German Ministry of Education and Research (BMBF) and the Humboldt University Berlin who funded the research for the present study as part of the project "Hyderabad as a Megacity of Tomorrow: Climate and Energy in a Complex Transition towards Sustainable Hyderabad – Mitigation and Adaptation Strategies by Changing Institutions, Governance Structures, Lifestyles and Consumption Patterns" (www.sustainable-hyderabad.de). In particular, we would like to thank Prof. Markus Hanisch for his guidance and support.

For data collection and data entry work we were supported by Kishore Rao, Pareekshit Suri Sarma, Purnima A. Kumar, Harshal Deshmukh, Hannelore Dicsi, Nikhil Rele, Vinita, Kim Campbell, Venkatesh Narasanna, Arpit Bansal and Mehul Khare. Further, we especially thank all interview respondents and other informants for their time and patience in answering our questions and sharing data. We are also obliged to Bombay Connect and ISB Learning Resource Centre for providing a productive working environment. Finally, we gratefully acknowledge the help of Catherine Peters and Vivek S. who provided proof-reading, editing and invaluable moral support during the last stages of completing this publication.

Foreword

It gives me great pleasure to write the foreword to *Organic Food Marketing in Urban Centres of India*. This book contains comprehensive and high quality research on organic food markets. It will be an invaluable resource document for the organic sector in India and globally.

India is rapidly emerging as one of the largest and fastest growing organic sectors in the world. This includes all facets of the sector, especially in terms of increases in production volumes, diversity of crops, the number of producers and the rapidly growing domestic consumer market to drive this growth. This trend is consistent with much of Asia and is being driven by the steady rise of the emerging middle classes who are concerned about food safety, particularly pesticides.

The book highlights many of the issues that come with emerging organic markets, such as supply chains with inconsistent production of inconsistent quality and the consumer confusion over the labelling of genuine organic products. This is a trend that comes with all organic markets as they emerge from a small base, however, by identifying the problems steps can be taken to remediate them.

The book's focus on urban markets is critically important. There is an old wise saying "Man does not live by bread alone."

Farmers, just like everyone else, need more than just a subsistence diet. They need to have an income so that they can send their children to school, pay for health care, veterinary care for their livestock, clothes, housing and other basic necessities.

The funds for these necessities of life must come from the trade of the produce that is surplus to their subsistence food needs. They need to have markets for their surplus produce so that they can earn the required money. If farmers cannot sell products for a profitable financial return, they lose money due to production expenditures.

Market diversity is the key. Organic markets need to cover all areas from short chain such as local farmer markets and local shops, direct to consumers such as Community-Supported Agriculture, regional markets with Participatory Guarantee Systems to national and international trade using third party certification systems.

The issue of local and urban markets featured in this book is very important for India's 547,591 certified organic farmers and PGS organic farmers. They utilise 1.1 million hectares which means that the average size of an Indian organic farm is 2 hectares. Most of them cannot access export markets due to the costs and economies of scale needed to do this. Local markets are the most appropriate for these farmers. Given that in 2012, for the first time in human history, 51% of people lived in cities, urban markets are the key to farm viability.

One key issue that was identified in the book is that many organic farmers are excluded from the premium markets because they are not third party certified, mostly due to the costs. This is becoming a critical issue and IFOAM is actively working on finding a range of appropriate solutions.

Trade is better than aid in ensuring food and income security as well as poverty reduction.

The critical issue is for producers to be able to choose the system that is most appropriate to their circumstances. For many producers, third party certification systems enable them to access high value regional, national and international systems. For others, particularly small holder farmers, the compliance costs can be higher than the financial returns so that PGS or consumer partnership systems are the most appropriate models. The key issue now is that farmers are able to choose the system that will bring them the greatest benefits. This is an important part ensuring that organic systems can be inclusive and available to all farmers.

While there is a great need for multiple markets from local through to international, the most important markets for small holder farmers are the local and domestic markets. *Organic Food Marketing in Urban Centres of India* contains high quality research that will make it a very useful resource tool for market development in India and for many other developing countries.

Andre Leu   February 28, 2013
President, IFOAM
a.leu@ifoam.org

1 Introduction

1.1 Context: The Booming Indian Organic Market?

In India, organic food has not yet grown beyond a small niche of the overall food market, despite recent claims that the market is "booming"[1]. While speaking of a boom might be an exaggeration at this stage, availability of organic products in urban markets has indeed grown significantly over the past ten years along with the growing demand by consumers. New organic stores open every month, and growing numbers of other shops and supermarkets have started to stock organic options. While nobody has officially measured the growth rate of organic food retailing, industry experts estimate it to be growing at 25-100%. Some retailers even claim growth figures of 100-300% over recent years.

In 2006, ICCOA commissioned a nation-wide survey of consumers published as *The Market for Organic Foods in India: Consumer Perceptions and Market Potential*. It detected considerable potential for developing the organic retail market, estimating the overall market potential in the eight largest cities of the country at INR 1,452 crore, and the accessible market potential through modern retail at INR 562 crore (Rao et al. 2006: 175).

Several trends which attest to the growth of the market simultaneously fuel its growth further. One of these trends is the concern over the new health crisis in India. While a large part of the population still suffers from undernourishment and infectious diseases, affluent urban dwellers increasingly develop non-communicable diseases like diabetes, heart disease and cancer that are primarily caused by food and lifestyle choices. These put a large burden of suffering, stress and health expenses on people. While pesticide residues in food are only one of the factors contributing to this unhealthy development, organic food can play an important role in shifting consumers to more healthy eating habits in general. For instance, organic products tend to be less processed and less refined than non-organic options. Wholesome products such as unpolished rice and millets tend to be more readily available in organic stores than

---

1 For instance, the July 2012 edition of Down To Earth magazine was titled "Organic Boom: Middle India takes a fancy to natural farming, but certification puts a spanner in its growth".

elsewhere. More generally, organic food is often part of more holistic lifestyles that also promote sensitivity to consumer choices in other areas.

Along with the spread of organic stores and growing health concerns, public discourse and media coverage of organic farming and food are also picking up. In the past, mainstream newspapers and online media only occasionally covered these topics. In June 2012, the popular television show Satyamev Jayate discussed the dangers of pesticide use and organic farming as an alternative. This marks an important shift: the large-scale entrance of organic issues into the mainstream media and public discourse. Some organic shop owners even speak of "Khanverts" – customers who discovered and "converted" to organic food in the wake of the television show hosted by the popular actor Aamir Khan. Concerns among the general public are growing over harmful health effects of pesticide residues in food, as well as of GMOs. Slowly, consumer awareness of organic is spreading beyond a limited segment of highly dedicated consumers and activists.

In urban centres, a diverse range of consumers far removed from agricultural production are now showing interest in reconnecting with the sources of their food. This phenomenon finds its expression in the increasing popularity of farmers markets and organic bazaars, community-supported agriculture schemes, consumer cooperatives and terrace gardening groups. While some of these initiatives are part of the grassroots organic movement, others were launched as commercial business ventures.

A small but growing number of health-conscious consumers are aware of organic food and willing to pay a premium, provided that products are readily available in consistent quality. However, while the popularity of organic has been growing significantly, organic retail is struggling with many obstacles, and is not developing at the rate that the industry hopes for. Whether the full potential of the organic sector will be realized in the future depends largely on sufficient production volumes combined with effective distribution and retailing.

The major challenges that producers, processors and retailers in the domestic market face include lack of a wide product range; consistent product availability, especially for fresh produce; quality control and difficulties in working with scattered producers; lack of institutional support and market linkages for small and marginal producers; supply chain constraints such as inadequate transport infrastructure, storage and cooling facilities; lack of awareness of organic food among consumers; and meeting consumer needs.

These challenges have to be addressed strategically in order to facilitate the growth of the organic sector, and to facilitate the participation of small and marginal farmers, who constitute over 80% of Indian farmers. In 2000, the Government of India introduced National Standards for Organic Production and a label for certified organic produce. However, agricultural policies and financial support continue to favour chemical-based farming. While some support for organic production is available, especially from the state governments, much of it is focused on export markets and is not accessible for smallholder producers. For instance, the bureaucratic requirements and cost of third-party certification are too high for most independent organic producers that sell in the domestic market. Also, the majority of consumers are not aware of the Indian organic label which has never been properly promoted in the domestic market. Organic farming support does not reach the majority of farmers practicing sustainable agriculture methods.

The spread of organic practices will be crucial for developing India's agriculture and food sector sustainably in the future. During the Green Revolution, tremendous gains in productivity of food grains were achieved – at the expense of the health of farmers and consumers as well as ecosystems, soil fertility and long-term productivity. Indiscriminate use of agro-chemicals and hybrid seeds have resulted in depleted soils, poisoned ground water, loss of biodiversity, deteriorating yields, indebted farmers and a growing disease burden. A large-scale spread of sustainable farming practices is the only way out of this agrarian crisis and the way forward for the sustainable development of the Indian agricultural sector. Some may see organic primarily as a business opportunity with excellent market prospects both internationally and domestically. Even more importantly, organic practices can ensure a sustainable future for millions of Indians whose livelihoods depend on farming and small and medium enterprises in food processing and retail.

India has a strong tradition and many strengths in organic farming. Despite the sweeping influence of chemical-based farming, traditional knowledge on sustainable farming practices still exists, and in remote areas of the country, chemical-free agriculture is still being practiced by default. The large number of small and marginal farmers in India could be a major strength in light of the fact that small farms have been found to be more productive (Altieri 2009), especially in organic farming systems. In the future, organic agriculture and other sustainable farming systems, together with organic food enterprises, will play an increasingly important role in the Indian economy. While higher revenues are currently achieved by exporting certified organic produce, the future growth of the organic segment will be influenced most significantly by developments in urban markets within India. Effective marketing of organic products in local, regional and national markets could make a major contribution to securing the livelihoods of smallholder producers, to strengthening small family farm structures and sustainable development of the country's food and agriculture sector.

1.2 Objectives of the Study

The organic market in India has been growing rapidly, and developments in the urban markets have been especially dynamic. While exports have been an important source of revenue for the organic sector, "the real opportunities of the growing community of organic producers (...) lie in the local and regional markets and to a smaller extent in the national channels" (Rao et al. 2006: IV). In light of this, it is important to get a better understanding of the structures of these domestic, regional and local markets.

The overall objective of this study is to examine the current state of the Indian domestic market for organic food and to provide an overview of different models of supply chain organization. It aims to shed more light on the challenges that stakeholders in organic value chains face, and point to successful solutions that they developed. This information will help facilitate the growth of the organic sector, with a focus on local and national markets.

The domestic market is highly diverse and fragmented, with vast differences in terms of supply chain reach, ownership of farmer producers, involvement of consumers and environmental impact. These differences need to be better understood in order to facilitate an optimal and sustainable growth of the organic sector which will benefit the bulk of small and marginal producers of India.

Towards this overall objective, the study has four specific objectives:

- to identify and classify the systems of production, distribution and marketing of organic food that exist in the major urban markets of South and West India;

- to identify obstacles in organic marketing and challenges to sustainable growth of the domestic market for organic products;

- to document lessons learned and best-practice examples for the benefit of farmers and farmer initiatives, food processors, organic companies, traders and retailers; and

- to provide a reference for policy makers in order to enable interventions that help develop the market for organic products in India in a sustainable manner.

This study provides a snapshot of the current state of the organic food sectors in three major urban markets of South and West India: Mumbai, the largest consumer market in the region with a strong organic movement; Bangalore, a dynamic IT-city with a large number of organic stores; and Hyderabad, whose market for organic food is considerably smaller and younger than the other two. Using the examples of successful marketing initiatives in various branches of the organic sector – including for instance smallholder producer companies, community-supported agriculture, large organic brands and organized retail chains – we draw conclusions and derive recommendations for building successful and sustainable organic food networks.

Our analysis covers third-party certified organic and PGS Organic as well as NPM[2] and non-certified products sourced by NGOs and retailers on the basis of short and transparent supply chains, personal relationships and trust. While these informal, trust-based relationships constitute a grey area to a certain extent, non-certified organic production makes up a significant share of total organic production and marketing in India, and can therefore not be ignored in any study of the country's organic sector. While this study focuses mainly on three cities in the South and West regions of India, the best-practice examples and lessons learned can and should be transferred to stakeholders across India.

---

2 Definitions see Chapter 3.1.

2 Analytical Approach and Methodology

2.1 Scope of the Study

This study examines three major urban markets of South and West India: Mumbai, Bangalore and Hyderabad. It builds upon two smaller studies that were previously conducted in Hyderabad in the context of the project "Hyderabad as a Megacity of Tomorrow: Climate and Energy in a Complex Transition towards Sustainable Hyderabad – Mitigation and Adaptation Strategies by Changing Institutions, Governance Structures, Lifestyles and Consumption Patterns" (www.sustainable-hyderabad.de). The first of these studies explored the current state of the market and future marketing opportunities for organic food products in Hyderabad (Osswald and Dittrich 2009). The second study looked at consumer awareness of organic food and food consumption in relation to environment, society and health in Hyderabad (Osswald and Dittrich 2010).

These explorative studies revealed that Hyderabad is a nascent organic market with a relatively small number of organic retail outlets and limited availability of organic foods in modern retail. The present study expands the scope to include two other urban markets that have more developed organic food sectors. Mumbai was selected because it is the largest and wealthiest consumer market in the South and West regions of India (Roy et al. 2010), and has the highest estimated potential for organic food sales (Rao et al. 2006). Mumbai also has a large number of organic stores, and several pioneer organic companies and retailers. Bangalore, surprisingly, has an even greater number of organic outlets per inhabitant than Mumbai, and the city has several long-standing organic stores as well as a large estimated market potential for organic food.

Primary data collection for the present study covered nearly all organic companies and marketing organizations in the three cities, most organic specialty stores, restaurants and catering enterprises that use organic ingredients, and a selection of other retailers that sell organic food products. A total of 103 outlets were surveyed, in addition to numerous outlets we visited which, upon investigation, never sold organic products, no longer stocked them or had closed down. A total of 82 interviews were conducted with representatives of 73 different organic companies, retailers and traders.

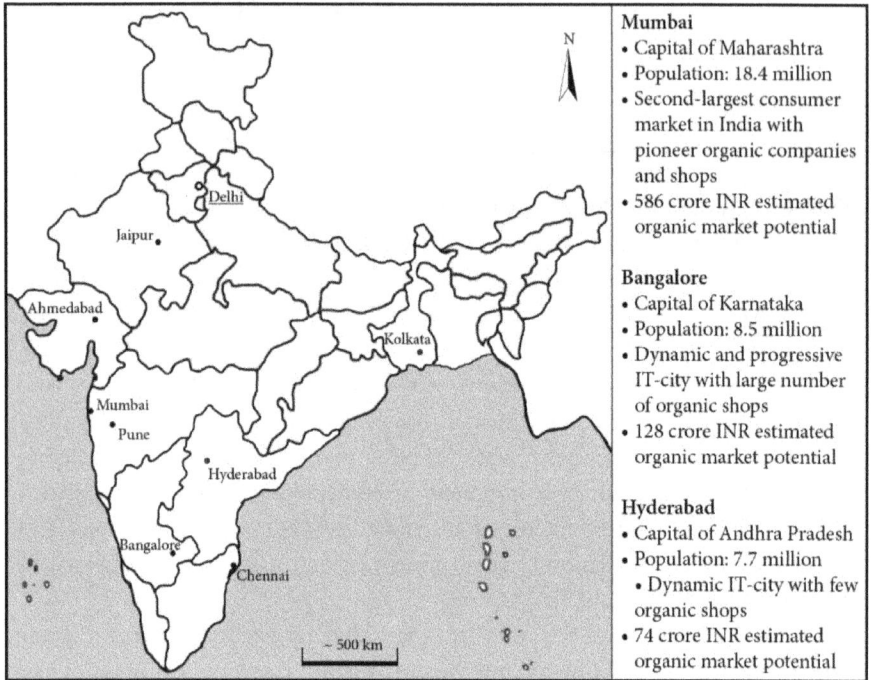

Mumbai
- Capital of Maharashtra
- Population: 18.4 million
- Second-largest consumer market in India with pioneer organic companies and shops
- 586 crore INR estimated organic market potential

Bangalore
- Capital of Karnataka
- Population: 8.5 million
- Dynamic and progressive IT-city with large number of organic shops
- 128 crore INR estimated organic market potential

Hyderabad
- Capital of Andhra Pradesh
- Population: 7.7 million
- Dynamic IT-city with few organic shops
- 74 crore INR estimated organic market potential

Figure 2-1: Overview map of the three cities covered by this study and the top eight metros studied in Rao et al. (2006)

Cartography: Nina Osswald; Population figures: Census 2011, Government of India, Office of the Registrar General and Census Commissioner, see http://censusindia.gov.in/

2.2 Study Design and Research Methodology

Data for this study was collected during 2011 and 2012 in several phases. As a first step, a comprehensive inventory of organic retail outlets and other marketing channels in the selected cities was mapped (cf. Osswald and Dittrich 2010), and organic food availability was recorded in a database. Data for this inventory was gathered by transect walks across the cities and compiled from existing databases such as the Directory of Organic Stakeholders published by ICCOA (Menon et al. 2009).

In addition to outlet surveys, representatives of stakeholders from the groups of sellers – such as retail chains, individual retailers, producer marketing initiatives, consumer cooperatives and delivery schemes – as well as suppliers – such as organic companies and producer groups – were interviewed. Interviews were semi-structured and qualitative, using interview guidelines, audio-recording and transcription. The first objective of these interviews was to classify existing organic marketing models according to their size and scope, ownership, production base, distribution model and supply chain organization, market orientation, retail model and product range. These criteria will be outlined in Chapter 4.1. The second objective of the interviews was to gather more in-depth information about the future development of the concerned organization, challenges in marketing organic foods, success factors and lessons learned, and sustainability issues. This data provided a guide on successful business strategies, infrastructure requirements, and policies that would facilitate marketing of organic products and a sustainable growth of the sector.

Table 2-1: Sample size of outlet surveys and interviews with organic stakeholders

City	Outlet surveys	Interviews
Mumbai	44	28
Bangalore	44	31
Hyderabad	15	15
Pune	0	1
India-wide operators	n/a	7
TOTAL	103	82

Secondary data collected from organic companies, NGOs and research institutes was used to complement the data from our own survey. An extensive review of the existing literature – academic book publications, journals, grey literature published by NGOs, newspaper articles and online publications – on the Indian market for organic food was also included in this study. The bibliography at the end of this book provides a comprehensive overview of the literature on the organic food sector in India to date, which – to our knowledge – is nearly complete in terms of book publications and academic journals and highly comprehensive in terms of grey literature, newspaper articles and online publications.

2.3 Limitations and Need for Further Research

Due to capacity limitations in the research phase, the scope of this study is focused on three urban centres in the South and West regions, even though the markets of Chennai, Pune and Ahmedabad were found to have equal organic sales potential by Rao et al. (2006). One case study from Pune of a pioneering community-supported agriculture initiative was included because of its innovative and successful approach to organic vegetable marketing, which can serve as a role model for other cities. Auroville might also have been included in the study; although it is not a major urban market, it has a relatively large number of organic farms, organic consumers, and community-supported agriculture schemes. The study did not cover stakeholders on the production level, except to a small extent in those cases where organic companies and organizations had their own production base, for instance in the case of producer companies.

The exact number of supermarket outlets that stock organic products could not be determined in this study because sufficient information was not available from most retail chains. The activities of organized retailers in organic food marketing could be investigated as part of a future study on a larger scale.

Further research on consumer awareness and demand for organic products in India is needed. Particularly, in light of the current discussion on mandatory certification for domestic marketing, it is important to get a clearer picture on how important certification is for consumers as opposed to personal relationships and trust in specific organizations, retailers and brands. Beyond the scope of this research project, these questions should be investigated as part of a large-scale, representative consumer study.

Furthermore, case studies on the production level would contribute to a better understanding of how participation in organic supply chains affects farmers. For this study, we relied on information provided by organic companies and marketing organizations on the benefits for their suppliers and member farmers. An independent study would show whether participation in organic supply chains benefits farmers with regard to improved revenue and farm viability, working conditions, and access to extension services. It would also shed more light on the perceptions and priorities of farmers.

3 The Organic Sector
in India

3.1 Sustainable Agriculture: Definitions

A number of different farming systems and techniques can be grouped under the umbrella of sustainable agriculture. All of these systems have in common that they reduce or avoid chemical pesticides and fertilizers, reject genetically modified organisms and work with natural cycles in order to manage pests and improve soil fertility. In this chapter, we give a brief overview of organic farming and other farming systems that are commonly cited considered as sustainable agriculture.

The most basic definition of organic agriculture is the cultivation of crops without chemical pesticides, synthetic fertilizers or genetically-modified organisms. Organic farmers rely primarily on renewable resources and on-farm inputs such as compost, manure and bio-pesticides. Soil fertility is maintained and pests are managed through alternative strategies, such as crop rotation, crop diversification, cultivation of legumes, and mechanical or biological pest control. Organic livestock is reared on organically grown fodder, without the use of antibiotics or growth hormones. In organic food processing, no ionizing radiations, food additives or growth promoters are allowed. More than an inventory of techniques, organic agriculture is intended as a holistic and systemic approach to agriculture:

> "Organic agriculture is a production system that sustains the health of soils, ecosystems and people. It relies on ecological processes, biodiversity and cycles adapted to local conditions, rather than the use of inputs with adverse effects. Organic agriculture combines tradition, innovation and science to benefit the shared environment and promote fair relationships and a good quality of life for all involved." (Definition by IFOAM[3])

Many countries all over the world have designed policies to regulate and standardize the farming techniques that are officially recognized as organic. In India, national organic standards and a certification scheme were established in

---

3 See online: www.ifoam.org/growing_organic/definitions/doa/

2000. Under the National Programme for Organic Farming, third-party certification is currently mandatory only for exports. Such a regulation has also been notified for the domestic market, but is yet to be implemented (see Chapter 3.3). Non-regulated sustainable agriculture systems, many of which consist of traditional and locally adapted techniques, play an equally or – as far as the domestic market is concerned – even larger role than certified organic production. Among the sustainable farming systems discussed in this chapter, organic is the only one that has a legal framework backing its standards, certification and labelling.

There are also private-sector regulations for organic production, one of the largest being bio-dynamic agriculture and the associated Demeter certification. Bio-dynamic agriculture is a system of organic agriculture that views the farm as a living, holistic organism, emphasizing the interrelationships of soil, plants and animals as a self-sustaining system and aiming to enhance, rejuvenate and maintain soil quality. Founded on the teachings of Rudolf Steiner, the name "bio-dynamic" refers to "working with the energies which create and maintain life" (Pfeiffer, no year). The Demeter certification program was established in 1928 as the first label for organically grown crops. Demeter International is the international bio-dynamic standards and certification group for products from bio-dynamic farming.

One of the non-regulated sustainable agriculture systems implemented in different localities in India is non-pesticide management (NPM). Less strict than organic, NPM focuses primarily on eliminating the use of synthetic pesticides. It relies on several techniques that are also used in organic farming, such as home-made concoctions of neem, garlic and chilli extracts, cow dung and cow urine as well as pheromone traps and other traditional methods of pest control (Misra 2009: 33). While some initiatives see NPM as a first stage on the way to certified organic production, others primarily aim to reduce exposure to pesticides for farmers. Since farmers spend a lot on synthetic pesticides, NPM also helps them cut costs while maintaining good yields, thereby raising overall farm profitability.

Other sustainable farming systems that share key characteristics of organic farming, and are practiced throughout India, include natural farming, low external input sustainable agriculture (LEISA), permaculture and Natueco farming[4]. While these farming systems play an important role in the

---

4   For a brief overview of these and several other sustainable farming systems, see Alvares 2009: 88. For a portrait of the Fukuoka natural farming practitioner Bhaskar Save, see Mansata 2010.

development of viable, food secure farms and sustainable agricultural production systems, their contribution to the organic food supply in major cities of India is currently negligible. Similarly, large parts of India that were never affected by the Green Revolution on a significant scale, and where traditional farming systems are still being practiced, are often considered as "organic by default". However, these remote areas are not well connected to markets, and their agricultural products cannot be officially marketed as organic (cf. Chapter 3.2 and 3.3).

A number of other farming systems are sometimes considered to be forms of sustainable agriculture, although the extent to which they really qualify as such is under intense debate (UNEP/ UNCTAD 2008: 6). In particular, integrated farming systems, although less strict than organic, can significantly reduce the need for synthetic inputs. Variants include Integrated Nutrient Management (INM), Integrated Pest and Disease Management (IPDM) and Integrated Weed Management (IWM). Integrated Pest Management, for instance, is based on the principle that pests should be managed rather than disruptively destroyed (see for example Prasad 2008). Both NPM and Integrated Farming Systems are sometimes viewed as a compromise between organic and intensive chemical-based agriculture or as a temporary stage for farms that are in conversion to organic.

All of the above-mentioned cultivation systems are, to varying degrees, more environmentally, economically and socially sustainable than conventional, chemical-based farming. In India, where resource-poor smallholder producers dominate the agriculture sector, this is especially true. An analysis based on case studies of different farming systems concluded that organic farming systems are superior to conventional agriculture both in terms of their productivity and their sustainability. While organic farming is not the only farming system that uses sustainable techniques, it is "unique in the sense that it offers a strategy which systematically integrates most of [... the sustainable techniques] in a farming system" (Kotschi and Müller-Sämann 2004: 9). It also has the advantage of reliability and transparency because of its compulsory standards and regulated mechanisms of inspection and certification. At the same time, organic farming is not necessarily more sustainable than other farming systems in every respect. The scale of a farm, its degree of mechanization and the complexity of its supply chains all have an impact on energy consumption and emissions. While organic farming overall uses significantly less energy than conventional farming (Ziesemer 2007), organic food produced on an industrial scale can have an equal or even greater ecological footprint[5] than non-organic food. In India, widespread mechanization could achieve a 10-20% increase in yield, but at the cost of an extra 43-260% in energy consumption (Pretty 1995, cited in Kotschi and Müller-Sämann 2004).

What follows is a brief summary of the most important reasons why organic farming is more sustainable than conventional agriculture[6]. Firstly, growing food organically benefits soils, water cycles and biodiversity. The author T. Singh (2004) writes that the Green Revolution technology "has been very successful in achieving spectacular results in food grain production during the last three decades. However, signs of fatigue in the natural resources have already emerged and have unleashed various agro-ecological problems. It has badly damaged the natural resource base of the country." (ibid: 1) Organic agriculture, by contrast, improves soil fertility and its properties, such as microbial biomass, microbial enzyme activity, earthworms and insect life, soil aggregate stability, water content and water holding capacity. A global-level comparative analysis of different studies revealed that organic farms have 30% greater species diversity than conventional farms and 50% more beneficial insects such as bees (Niggli 2010). Overall, sustainable agriculture strengthens ecosystem linkages and promotes their healthy functioning. It also maintains natural ecosystem services, such as nutrient cycling, pest regulation and pollination.

Secondly, sustainable agriculture can significantly reduce fossil fuel consumption and make an important contribution to climate change mitigation and adaptation[7]. Agriculture and diet are among the main contributors to global greenhouse gas emissions: In the 1990s, approximately 15% have been due to agricultural land use (Cole et al. 1997). Most of the global nitrous oxide emissions as well as roughly two thirds of methane emissions originate from agriculture (Kotschi and Müller-Sämann 2004). Organic agriculture, by contrast, can contribute significantly to the reduction of greenhouse gas emissions[8] because it uses less fossil fuel – a major source of

---

5   For an introduction to the concept of ecological footprints, see Wackernagel and Rees (1996).

6   A more comprehensive overview of the advantages of organic agriculture can be found in J. Singh (2004: 281–3), and Scialabba (2010).

7   For a more detailed account of the climate impact of different farming systems than we can provide here, see Niggli et al. 2009; Niggli and Fließbach 2009; Foodwatch 2008; von Koerber and Juergen Kretschmer 2009; von Koerber et al. 2009.

8   For an overview of direct and indirect reduction on agricultural greenhouse gas emissions in organic agriculture see Kotschi and Müller-Sämann 2004: 37, Table 14.

carbon dioxide emissions in agriculture. On average, organic farms consume 30-70% less energy per unit of land. For instance, not only is the production of synthetic fertilizers highly energy-intensive, it also cost the Government of India INR 61,000 crore of subsidies in 2011 (according to Dr. A.K. Yadav). Organic farms do not use synthetic inputs, and they tend to be less mechanized, thereby saving energy on machines and transport. Greenhouse gas emissions of methane and nitrous oxide are also lower in organic farming. Methane, which originates mostly from enteric fermentation in livestock, from wetlands and from paddy cultivation, is reduced through limiting the number of farm animals per area, changing livestock diet and applying smaller quantities of animal manure.

In addition to its ability to reduce greenhouse gas emissions, organic farming also minimizes nitrogen loss and improves the sequestration of carbon in soils by way of tight nutrient and energy cycles, long and diversified crop rotations, legume cropping, agroforestry and incorporation of manure and compost into the soil (Kotschi and Müller-Sämann 2004). Further, sustainable agriculture techniques make farms more resilient to extreme weather events and help farmers adapt to climate change. It reduces water requirements for applying fertilizers, increases water retention and percolation, and makes crops more drought tolerant. The cultivation of traditional crops that are adapted to the specific agro-climatic conditions in dryland areas contributes to making organic farms more resilient to climate change.

Thirdly, in addition to its environmental benefits, organic farming eliminates exposure to chemicals, which causes thousands of deaths and illnesses among Indian farmers each year (C. H. S. Rao et al. 2005; Prabu 2009). It also reduces the risk of chemical residues in food products, a particular concern in India, as it remains among the countries with the highest levels of toxic residues in food[9] in the world (Chander 1997; Ramanjaneyulu and Chennamaneni 2007; Sinha, M. V. V. Rao, and Vasudev 2012). A study conducted in 1996 by the Indian Council of Medical Research found that 51% of all food analyzed was contaminated with pesticide residues and that 20% was above tolerable levels (cited in Lohr and Dittrich 2007). In addition to reducing the adverse effects of exposure to synthetic pesticides, organic food has been found to be nutritionally superior, containing more vitamins and micronutrients such as polyphenoles and antioxidants than non-organic products grown under the same conditions (Niggli et al. 2007; www.quilf.org).

---

9 Cf. Ramanjaneyulu and Chennamaneni (2007) for an analysis of the institutional context of pesticide regulation in India, with special reference to vegetables in Hyderabad market.

Fourthly, organic farming is more efficient and economically viable than conventional farming (Kilcher 2007; DDS 2008; Lukas and Cahn 2008; Adhavani 2009), especially in countries like India where the majority of farms are small and resource-poor. Many of these farmers are highly indebted and depend on agrochemical corporations for chemical inputs and hybrid or GMO seeds. As a result of this debt crisis, 250,000 farmers committed suicide in India over the last ten years. Small organic farms are more diversified than large ones, which reduces the risk of crop failure due to pests or extreme weather events and vulnerability to market fluctuations. Organic farms use limited amounts of external inputs, such as biopesticides and biofertilizer, thereby reducing operational costs. Despite lower yields for some crops and in certain conditions, the total average yield and net profit is usually higher in the long run (J. Singh 2004; Eyhorn 2005). Studies cited by Niggli (2010) have shown that 100% conversion to organic farming would impact yields negatively by 20-40% in intensively farmed regions under best geo-climatic conditions, and by less than 20% in less favourable conditions. The author also refers to a comparative survey of 200 case studies (UNEP/ UNCTAD 2008) which found that organic farming can increase yields by as much as 116% in subsistence agriculture and in regions with periodic droughts and floods, as is the case in many parts of India.

3.2   Organic Production and Domestic Market Size

Estimates on how much area is under some form of organic cultivation in India vary widely, depending on the data source. There is no reliable system for documentation of non-certified organic farming, which means that data on cultivation area and production volumes is available only for certified organic produce. It can be assumed that the bulk of the total domestic production comes from non-certified sustainable production systems such as natural farming, bio-dynamic agriculture, NPM[10] and traditional farming systems.

Large parts of India, such as the Himalaya, the Deccan Plateau or the Adivasi area across Central India, were never significantly affected by Green Revolution technology. Farmers there still practice traditional ways of farming, without chemical pesticides and fertilizers. In addition, many farmers in dryland areas do not have access to irrigation and, as a result, do not use chemical fertilizers. According to Anshu and Mehta (no year), only one fifth of

---

10 Definitions see Chapter 3.1.

dry land farmers in India use chemical inputs at all. Opinions vary on whether the agricultural produce of these areas can be called "organic". While some stakeholders call these production systems "essentially organic" (Bhattacharyya 2004: 175), "organic by default" or "organic by tradition" (Menon, Sema, and Partap 2010), others argue that such claims do not have any scientific basis, and that crops grown on these farms should be marketed as organic. Some experts argue that using the term "organic by default" for these traditional farming systems is misleading because organic stands for more than just avoiding chemical inputs; rather, it involves a combination of traditional, locally-adapted farming knowledge with the techniques developed by modern science. The latter are absent in remote, traditional farming systems.

Nevertheless, traditional farming practices constitute a huge potential for India's organic sector, because these traditional farmers have retained a pool of knowledge on traditional and sustainable farming methods that have been lost in areas where industrial technology has dominated farming: "India has a rich heritage of agricultural traditions that are suitable for designing organic production systems." (Garibay and Jyoti 2003). Furthermore, land that has never been farmed chemically can be converted to organic more easily, and it would also be easier to integrate these farms into an organic production-marketing system than to convert farms that have been cultivated with chemicals. For instance, Menon, Sema, and Partap (2010) see a large potential in the fact that the farming systems in remote areas like the North East Indian Himalaya Region are, by and large, "practicing organic farming naturally" (ibid: 82). By contrast, some market experts argue that even if remote farmers use organic practices, the lack of verification and quality control prevents them from marketing their produce as organic. At present, traditional farms in remote areas have access only to local rural markets, so the question of whether their products might be marketed as "organic" on a larger scale does not arise.

The total cultivated area in India that is certified organic (see Chapter 3.3) is estimated at 1.02 million hectares (see Table 3-1). Additionally, organic food products are collected from over 3 million hectares of organic certified wild collection area. This is about 0.7% of total cultivable land area. Based on these figures, India ranks thirty-third in terms of total land under organic cultivation, and eighty-eighth for organic production area compared to total farming area (OTA 2010). The leading states in terms of organic production area are Madhya Pradesh, Himachal Pradesh, Rajasthan, Maharashtra, Uttar Pradesh and Uttarakhand (Jishnu and Sood 2012).

India may have only a small share of the total 37 million hectares of cultivated organic land globally in 2010 (IFOAM & FibL); however, of 1.6 million organic farmers worldwide, between 400,551 (Willer and Kilcher 2012) and 1 million (Jishnu and Sood 2012) are in India, which makes it the country with the largest number of organic producers. The number of farmers registered with certification agencies is somewhere between 500,000 (Oneindia 2010) and 714,000 (Menon et al. 2009). Over 80% of the cultivated land under certification process is cultivated by grower groups, and the remainder belongs to individual farmers. According to APEDA figures, there were 1,226 individual growers and 1,831 farmer groups in 2011.

Between 2003/04 and 2009, the area under certified organic farming was expanded from less than 42,000 hectares to 400,000 hectares certified and another 400,000 under conversion (Menon, Sema, and Partap 2010; Menon et al. 2009). By 2011, it had grown to over 1 million hectares (see Table 3-1), and it is expected to further increase over the coming years. In a presentation at BioFach India 2011, the former Director of National Centre for Organic Farming, Dr. A.K. Yadav, mentioned that the target is to expand certified production area to 3 million hectares and the number of certified organic producers to 1 million.

Bio-dynamic cultivation is currently being practiced on 504 Demeter certified farms on 5,882 hectares (BDAI 2012). Most of this is tea, coffee, spices and basmati rice for export markets. There is no data available about bio-dynamic producers who are not Demeter certified and registered with BDAI.

The total organic production volume in 2010-11 was 3.88 tonnes or 1% of total agricultural production, according to both the Ministry of Agriculture and APEDA. Jishnu and Sood (2012) by contrast cite a figure of only 2.85 million tonnes.

The value of certified organic production again varies between different data sources, as Table 3-1 shows. A credible estimate of INR 5,640 crore of total organic production during 2009-10 comes from Dr. A.K. Yadav. In 2010-11, this grew to INR 8,000 crore, nearly 50% of which was marketable surplus. The differences in these estimates are likely due to the fact that different stakeholders collect and compile information and data at different points in time, and using various methods. Certification agencies submit all their data annually to APEDA, the authority that functions as secretariat of the National Accreditation Board and sets the organic standards. However, APEDA does not share or publish this compiled information periodically. Thus the task of compiling data from various sources and analyzing, researching and publishing it is left to other agencies.

Table 3-1: Organic production and marketing data overview

Data source [1]	APEDA	Ministry of Agriculture [2]	ICCOA estimate	OTA 2010
Total organic area, certified and in conversion	4.43 million ha (1 million ha cultivation, and 3.43 million ha wild collection)	4.34 ha (0.78 million ha cultivation, and 3.56 million ha wild collection)	1.02 million ha certified cultivation, and several hundred thousand ha in conversion	1.18 million ha total acreage (2009-10)
Total organic production, certified and in conversion	3.88 million tonnes (including processed and value added food products, excluding cotton)	3.88 million tonnes / INR 5,640 crore (2009-10), and INR 8,000 crore INR (2010-11, of which INR 4,000 crore marketable surplus)		400,000 tonnes INR 4,000 crore
Organic export sales	70,000 tonnes / INR 839 crore (2011-12), and INR 1,027 crore organic textiles; expected INR 2,000 crore for food in 2012-13	n/a	INR 840 crore food products, and INR 1,025 crore organic cotton (2012)	n/a
Domestic market sales	n/a	INR 1,000 crore	INR 300 crore (2011-2012), INR 600 (2012-13)	n/a

(1) All data 2010-11 unless specified otherwise; all data including cotton unless specified otherwise

(2) Cited in Jishnu & Sood 2012, and information given by Dr. A.K. Yadav, former Director of National Centre for Organic Farming (NCOF)

Until recently, the bulk of Indian organic production went into export markets: about 70% according to Carroll (2005), and as much as 85% of sales according to Garibay and Jyoti (2003). This is a result of a combination of various interlinked factors. Firstly, there is a lack of awareness and demand among consumers in the domestic market. Secondly, government policies for organic farming in the past and present have been strongly export-oriented. And thirdly, world market prices for organic products are much higher than for non-organic products; about 20-30% higher according to Carroll (2005), and more than twice as much based on figures cited by Jishnu and Sood (2012).

Of the total organic production in India, 70,000 tonnes went into export in 2010-11, registering a 33% growth over the previous year (APEDA 2012). According to Willer and Kilcher (2012), exports grew by 20% in 2011. Organic exports were worth over INR 800 crore in 2011-12 (see Table 3-1). APEDA forecast that exports would double again in 2012-13 (Foodnavigator Asia 2012). Exports are to be expanded to INR 5,000 crore by 2015 (Heinze 2012).

By comparison, domestic organic sales already add up to 240,000 tonnes at a value of INR 1,000 crore, including cotton (Jishnu and Sood 2012). While according to Dr. A.K. Yadav, the value of total marketable surplus organic production in India was INR 4,000 crore in 2010-11, domestic sales of organic food products totalled only INR 400-420 crore. Sales of organic cotton by farmers to domestic industries amounted to another INR 580-600 crore. ICCOA expects the total trade in organic products from and within India to touch INR 5,500 crore in the next four years. The growth of organic food exports, domestic market sales and textiles exports since 2005 is shown in Figure 3-1.

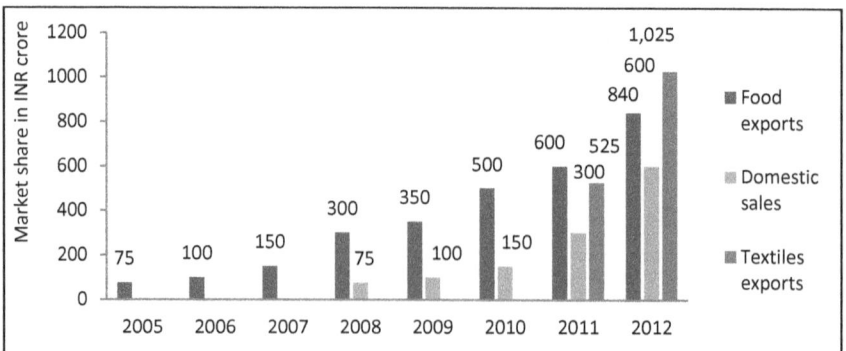

Figure 3-1: Growth of export and domestic market shares since 2005

Source: ICCOA, estimates compiled from various sources

Along with the recent growth of organic production volumes and number of organic companies, the organic food retail scene in Indian metropolitan areas is experiencing a phase of dynamic development. Some analysts even speak of "a real boom" (Eyhorn 2005: 74; Jishnu and Sood 2012). Industry experts estimate the growth of domestic sales over the past few years at 25-30%, while some retailers claim growth figures of 100-300%. About half of the organic stores in our survey reported substantial growth of sales in recent years, and the other half at least slight growth. None had suffered a decline or stagnation in sales. Research and Markets (2011) in their "Indian Organic Food Market Analysis" anticipates a compound annual growth rate of the organic sector of 15%.

By now, over 1,000 different organic products are available in the domestic market (Blume 2012). The products most frequently demanded in organic quality by Indian consumers are vegetables and fruits, followed by spices, rice, pulses and tea (Garibay and Jyoti 2003; Rao et al. 2006). Within India, the major markets for certified organic products are in the metropolitan areas, especially Delhi, Mumbai, Kolkata, Chennai, Bangalore and Hyderabad.

According to APEDA, there are approximately 2,000 shops selling organic products in India, in addition to a large and growing number of conventional supermarkets that also stock organic. Another source estimates the number of retail outlets selling organic products at 2,500, and the number of consumers buying organic at least occasionally at 1 million (Oneindia 2010). According to an estimate by Dr. A.K. Yadav, domestic sales comprised INR 200 crore of sales in approximately 200 outlets of organized retail chains, and INR 220 crore in approximately 2,000 small shops and farmer retail outlets in 2010-11.

A large number of organic outlets opened up in recent years, and more and more conventional food stores both in general trade and organized modern retail have started stocking organic products. Some of them shut down again or stopped selling organic products after a while due to different reasons, ranging from lack of customers, supply problems or lack of economic viability. Nevertheless, overall availability of organic products continues to improve rapidly. New organic stores, organic online retailers and other delivery initiatives open up in the big cities almost on a monthly basis. The main drivers of this growth are rising incomes of the middle classes as well as a general trend towards health-consciousness. Half of the respondents interviewed by Osswald and Dittrich (2010) started buying organic products less than one year ago, and several experts expect that the share of the population that buys organic food will grow to about 4% over the next ten years.

These growth figures notwithstanding, the full potential of the organic sector in India is far from being realized. The bulk of 84% of the total production is sold in the domestic market as conventional, without any organic premium. This is largely due to a lack of adequate market linkages and organic marketing channels. Organic farmers are missing out on a huge untapped potential; according to Jishnu and Sood (2012) over INR 4,000 crore per year. Many market analysts, marketers and NGOs expect the demand for organic food within India to rise significantly in the near future. Rao et al. (2006) estimated the overall domestic market potential in the eight largest cities alone at INR 1,452 crore, and at INR 2,100 crore for the entire country. According to Menon, Sema, and Partap (2010), organic food can capture 5-6% of the total food market in the mid- to long-term, and the Associated Chambers of Commerce and Industry of India estimate that the domestic organic sector can grow to INR 10,000 crore by 2015 (Assocham 2011).

3.3   Institutional Context and Regulations

The Indian Ministry of Commerce launched the National Programme for Organic Production (NPOP) in 2000 (Government of India 2000), laying down the National Standards for Organic Products (NSOP, see Government of India 2005). These standards regulate production, processing, labelling, storage and transport as well as inspection and certification procedures for organic products. They form the basis of certified organic production in India. Under the NPOP framework, a national organic label (see Figure 3-2) was developed, which is awarded to producers who are inspected and certified by one of the nationally accredited certification agencies for compliance with the organic standards. At present, there are 24 certification agencies accredited under NPOP[11].

The official India Organic label can be found on all organic products that are exported, and many branded products sold domestically in organic stores and supermarkets. At present, it is used mainly by large-scale and export-oriented operators. For export of organic products, a producer or processor has to be third-party certified by one of the 24 certification agencies currently accredited under NPOP, and the India Organic label has to be displayed on the

---

11 See Table 8-1 for a full list of certification agencies operating in India in 2012.

product packaging. Many export-oriented organic companies are certified under the Indian as well as US and European organic standards. For the domestic market, the NPOP was notified under the APGMC Act (Agricultural Produce Grading, Marking and Certification Act), but use of the label is still voluntary. The term "organic" is not legally protected for use in retail, and organic produce can also be sold without certification. FSSAI is currently in the process of notifications of organic rules for the domestic market.

Figure 3-2: Official India Organic label for products certified according to NSOP (National Standards for Organic Production)

Source: APEDA

This system of third-party certification guarantees organic production standards and product quality to consumers who are far removed from the farm level. For producers and companies selling to export markets or organized retailers, it is important to be certified and display the organic label on the product packaging. At the same time, third-party certification has been criticized by Indian sustainable agriculture organizations as too much oriented towards exports, and not viable for the majority of small and marginal farmers in India. While the organic label would give small farmers equal access to organic markets and organic premiums, certification is not easily accessible for most farmers that grow for local markets (Carroll 2005). The fees as well as documentation requirements are discussed as the main obstacles that stop them from applying for certification (Garibay and Jyoti 2003, cf. Chapter 5.5).

In order to provide an alternative to third-party certification for small organic farmers, civil society organizations like rural development NGOs and farmer cooperatives around the world developed Participatory Guarantee Systems (PGS). These are local-level quality assurance systems, working with group certification by way of a system of participation and peer monitoring. Globally, approximately 40 PGS initiatives have been established which vary in terms of their methodology and approach, but which all share common principles and values; above all, the participation and ownership of smallholder producers in all stages of the certification process. PGS are often linked to producer companies, NGO-supported marketing initiatives, and localized approaches to marketing such as consumer-producer cooperatives. India is one of the leading countries in terms of the number of farmers working with PGS (Willer and Kilcher 2012).

Figure 3-3: PGS (Participatory Guarantee System) Organic label awarded by the PGS Organic India Council

Source: PGS Organic India Council

In India, the PGS India Organic Council developed the PGS Organic label (see Figure 3-3) in cooperation with the Food and Agricultural Organisation (FAO) and the Ministry of Agriculture, Government of India (Rao 2006). This label is used for marketing in the domestic market, and it "certifies sustainably grown organic farm crops that are built on the foundations of quality, trust and alliance through a farmer's social network" (PGS India Organic Council Brochure). Several organizations market their produce under the PGS label, including Deccan Development Society, Timbaktu Organic and Keystone Foundation (Alvares 2009).

Parallel to the PGS grassroots movement led by PGS India Organic Council and Organic Farming Association of India (OFAI), the Government of India through National Centre of Organic Farming (NCOF) is planning to operate a separate PGS initiative. The operational structure is based on farmer groups who are the main operational and decision-making unit. These farmer groups are supervised and their decisions endorsed by a regional council, which is in turn headed by a zonal council. The supervising bodies are NCOF and National Advisory Committee at the Department of Agriculture and Cooperation.

NCOF developed two labels for PGS certified products that are either in conversion (PGS-India Green, see Figure 3-4) or fully organic (PGS-India Organic). NCOF sees PGS-India not as a competitor or replacement for third-party certification system, but rather as a precursor to the third-party system, and as a tool for building the capacity of farmer groups to establish internal control systems (ICS).

Figure 3-4: PGS-India labels for in-conversion and fully organic products developed by NCOF

Source: Presentation by Dr. A.K. Yadav, former Director of National Centre for Organic Farming (NCOF), at BioFach India 2011

Although the Government of India supports organic farming on the policy level, some authors and organic sector representatives claim that there is no overall strategy for greening agriculture (Anshu and Mehta, no year) or for developing the domestic market for organic food. Government policies for organic have been skewed towards exports (Carroll 2005; Bhattacharyya 2004). Critics also complain that government policies and programmes are not well connected to the farm level, and do not reach the bulk of small and marginal farmers. The Department of Agriculture supports organic production mostly for large-scale farmers and for export markets (cf. Richter and Kovacs 2005; Singh 2004; Carroll 2005; IBEF 2004). At present, most support for small organic farmers with regard to training, extension services, information and marketing assistance is delivered by India's strong NGO sector (Garibay and Jyoti 2003; NAC Working Group 2013).

At the same time, the Government of India professed ambitious plans of increasing the total area under organic farming to five million hectares over the coming years (Yadav 2009), supported by funds from both national and federal state governments (Heinze 2012). The Government of India and the federal state governments encourage and support organic farming through various missions, schemes and programmes. The Ministry of Agriculture has the following specific missions and programmes that provide support to organic farming:

- Organic Farming Scheme, National Horticultural Mission (NHM)

- Rastriya Krishi Vikas Yojana (RKVY; National Agriculture Development Plan)

- National Centre for Organic Farming (NCOF)

These programs are to be proposed by the State Departments of Agriculture and Horticulture and are implemented by the federal state governments, either directly or through NGOs and farmer organizations as implementing agencies. Once a state department approves and proposes such a project in their state, the central government provides financial support.

The bulk of government support comes in the form of funds and schemes for farmers. Support is also available for attending trade fairs and for organizing trainings and workshops. Additionally, various commodity boards like Spices Board, Tea Board, Coffee Board and APEDA which come under the Union Ministry of Commerce provide financial support for organic certification, logistics and processing of organic production that is directed towards export. The Ministry of Food Processing also provides subsidies for establishing processing units.

The state governments overall have a more proactive stance towards organic agriculture than the central government (Alvares 2009). So far, eleven states have drafted organic farming policies. Sikkim was the first state to declare the objective of making the entire state fully organic by 2015. To this end, the Government of Sikkim launched a major Organic Mission in 2010, engaged service providers and companies and initiated organic certification of the state's entire 60,000 ha of land area. The states of Uttaranchal and Mizoram also declared their intention to become fully organic (OTA 2010). Others such as Arunachal Pradesh, Nagaland and Meghalaya are planning to follow their example (Menon, Sema, and Partap 2010).

Many state governments also provide direct support to farmers, farmer organizations and NGOs, although how much financial support is available for organic farming varies widely from one federal state to another. The Government of Karnataka earmarked INR 100 crore for establishing Biovillages in all districts across the state, and it allocated INR 13 crore for promoting organic production through technical training for farmers, infrastructure development, public awareness raising and opening of retail outlets (OTA 2010). The Government of Karnataka also established the Jaivik Krishik

Society as an association of farmer groups in order to provide production support and market access for small organic farmers.

In Andhra Pradesh, the semi-governmental agency SERP together with the government organization HACA launched the Community-Managed Sustainable Agriculture Programme as part of the the state-wide rural poverty reduction project "Indira Kranthi Patham". The organization assists farmers in implementing NPM production in 3,000 villages across 18 districts of Andhra Pradesh and facilitated the establishment of 300 NPM shops run by farming women's self-help groups (Misra 2009). The programme succeeded in bringing 1.5 million hectares of farmland under non-pesticide management cultivation, turning 124 villages entirely pesticide-free, and 26 villages fully organic. As a result, the Union Government saved INR 1.2 crore on fertiliser subsidies. Farmers cut down their expenses by INR 1.47 crore by eliminating pesticides and reducing fertiliser use (Jishnu and Sood 2012; Raidu and Ramanjaneyulu 2008; Ramanjaneyulu and Rao 2008). The programme works with a Participatory Guarantee System and also provides assistance to farmers who want to get organic third-party certification.

In addition to government and non-profit organizations, private-sector associations also support the development of the organic sector. For instance, the Indian Organic Trade Association was founded in 2010 with the goal of promoting organic production and marketing within India and for export. It is not fully functional yet, and the extent of this body's influence on the development of the domestic market remains to be seen. It is likely that the focus for some time to come will be mostly on promoting exports, because of the higher margins compared to selling domestically.

Other private-sector initiatives in India developed their own labelling systems, which are used either instead of or in addition to the official India Organic label. The retail chain Fabindia, for instance, developed a three-tier labelling system that distinguishes between so-called natural products, products from farms in conversion to organic, and fully certified organic products[12]. ICCOA designed a label for vegetables sourced regionally from Karnataka, from farms that are in conversion to organic, in order to enable farmers to better market their produce during the financially challenging conversion period (see Case Study 6). Another example is Navdanya; the NGO gives the "Navdanya Guarantee" for organically grown products, the credibility of which is based on the reputation of the NGO rather than on third-party certification.

---

12 See Singh 2009 and Case Study 2 for details.

Demeter International, a private-sector organizations that is responsible for the world-wide certification of bio-dynamic production, works closely with the Bio-dynamic Association of India (BDAI), a registered society whose mission is to spread and support bio-dynamic production in India, for instance through trainings. The bulk of Demeter certified produce from India is exported, and the Demeter label for bio-dynamic production has not been introduced to the Indian domestic market yet.

4 Organic Food Distribution Systems

4.1 Domestic Market Structures and Classification Framework

Many companies that operate in the domestic organic sector in India are very young (OTA 2010). It is only in the last ten to fifteen years that the first commercial organic companies started selling in the domestic market. Before that, the organic sector was largely divided into two strands: Export-oriented companies that work with large independent producers of certified products; and domestic marketing initiatives that work with small farmers directly or through NGOs (cf. Singh 2009). By now, a wide variety of organizational models for the production, processing, distribution and marketing of organic food products, both certified and non-certified, emerged in India's organic sector. One of the objectives of the present study was to provide a systematic overview of this diversity in order to better understand the functioning of various distribution models, and to assess their respective significance for the organic sector as a whole.

Based on a comprehensive survey of urban markets as well as on different classifications used by other authors and organic sector experts, we developed a framework for classifying all stakeholders in the Indian organic food sector. The set of criteria used to analyze the wide variety of organic food distribution systems in the domestic market is shown in Figure 4-1. The criteria for urban retail models are further differentiated in Figure 4-2. While this framework can be applied to all stakeholders including growers, processors, trading companies and retailers, the main focus in the ensuing analysis is on organic food retailing in urban centres. This chapter starts by providing an overview of the different systems of organic food production and supply chain organization that exist in India. The ensuing Chapters 4.2 to 4.7 focus mainly on urban retail.

An emerging organic market like India is structurally different from the well-developed organic markets in the USA or some European countries, where organic food is typically certified. Herrmann (2010) divides organic food retail

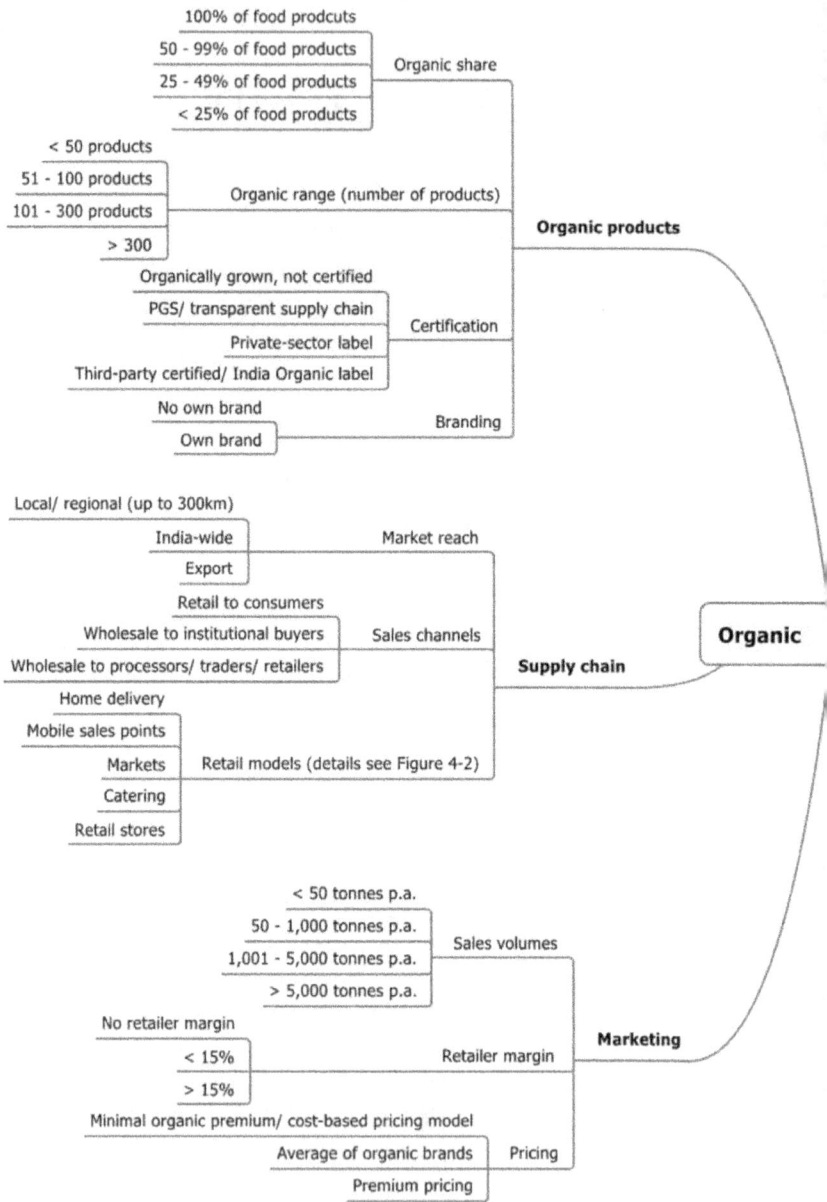

Figure 4-1: Classification criteria for stakeholders in the organic food sector

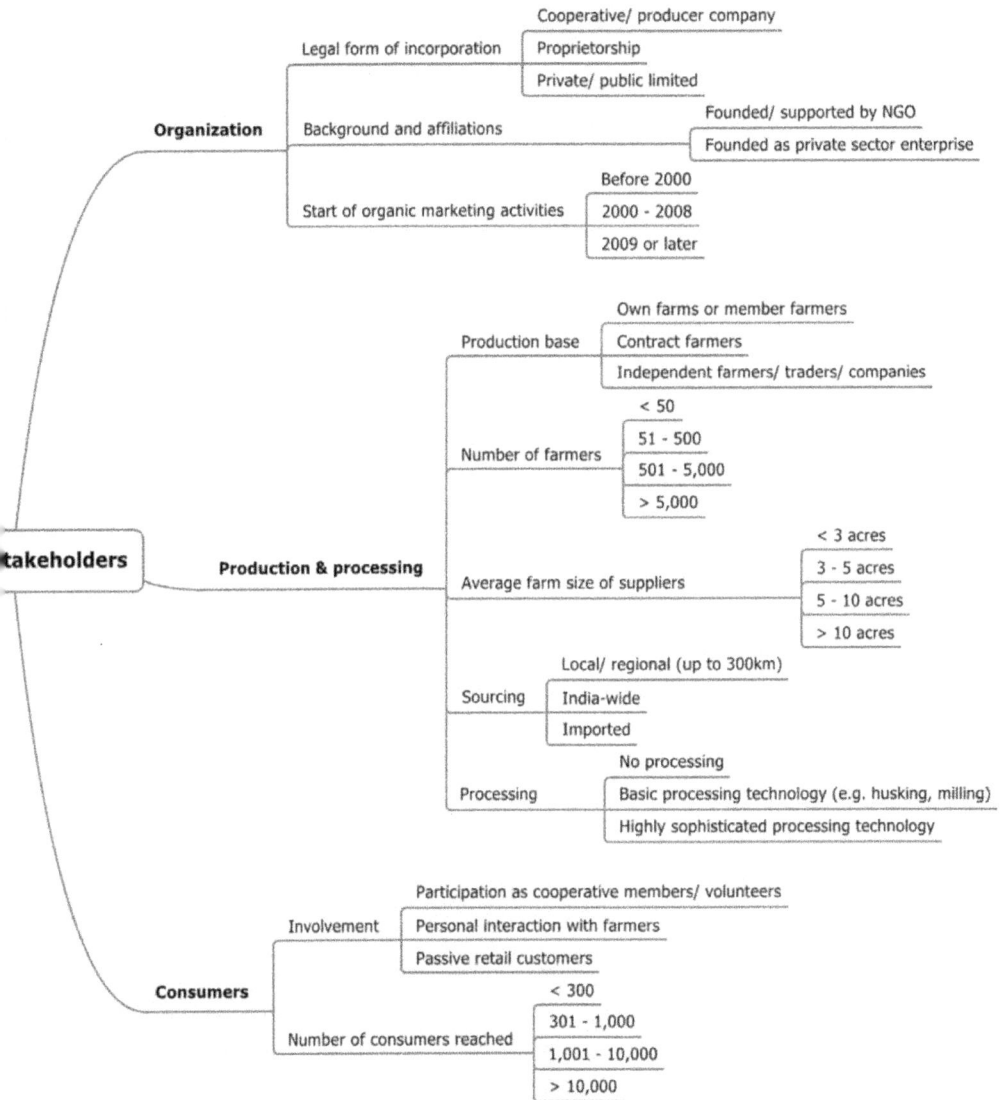

Stakeholders

Organization

- **Legal form of incorporation**
  - Cooperative/ producer company
  - Proprietorship
  - Private/ public limited
- **Background and affiliations**
  - Founded/ supported by NGO
  - Founded as private sector enterprise
- **Start of organic marketing activities**
  - Before 2000
  - 2000 - 2008
  - 2009 or later

Production & processing

- **Production base**
  - Own farms or member farmers
  - Contract farmers
  - Independent farmers/ traders/ companies
- **Number of farmers**
  - < 50
  - 51 - 500
  - 501 - 5,000
  - > 5,000
- **Average farm size of suppliers**
  - < 3 acres
  - 3 - 5 acres
  - 5 - 10 acres
  - > 10 acres
- **Sourcing**
  - Local/ regional (up to 300km)
  - India-wide
  - Imported
- **Processing**
  - No processing
  - Basic processing technology (e.g. husking, milling)
  - Highly sophisticated processing technology

Consumers

- **Involvement**
  - Participation as cooperative members/ volunteers
  - Personal interaction with farmers
  - Passive retail customers
- **Number of consumers reached**
  - < 300
  - 301 - 1,000
  - 1,001 - 10,000
  - > 10,000

in well-developed organic markets into conventional retailers, natural food stores and organic supermarkets. Conventional retailers are further subdivided into discount supermarkets, national and regional retail chains, independent retailers, and drugstores. Surendran (2010) classifies organic retail in India into four categories: modern format stores (supermarket chains), specialty stores, organic food marketers (organic companies who run their own branded stores), and direct marketing initiatives. The latter category includes only home deliveries by organic company, however, and not those by other types of stakeholders. Osswald and Dittrich (2010) distinguish four major categories: supermarkets, commercial organic stores, NGOs/ direct marketing and other formats (such as small health shops).

In our survey of the organic food sector in South and West India, we found that some of the categories that are relevant in other countries do not exist in India at all, such as exclusively organic supermarkets. At the same time, none of the above classifications proved sufficiently differentiated for our empirical findings. While the distinction between conventional, organized retailers and organic specialty retail is relatively clear-cut, there are a few other organizational forms and distribution channels as well as several mixed forms which are less easily classified. Figure 4-2 shows the main categories of organic food retailing in urban centres of India that emerged from our empirical survey.

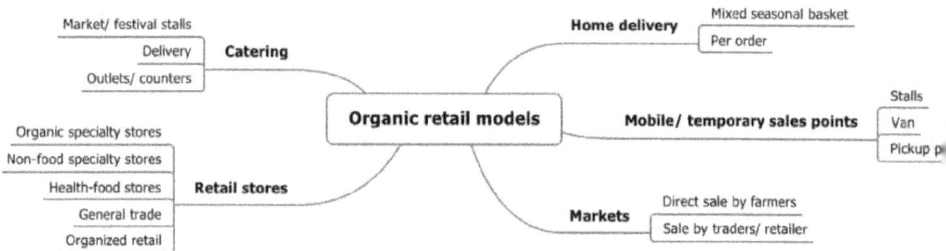

Figure 4-2: Organic retail models in urban centres

One way of classifying the stakeholders in India's diverse and fragmented organic sector is along a continuum from commercially oriented organic companies at one end, and farmer producer organizations and grassroots NGOs at the other. Over the past decades, organic smallholder producers in India were supported in their agricultural production activities mainly by civil society groups such as local grassroots and rural development NGOs (Alvares 2009). The primary interest of these NGOs is to support sustainable rural livelihoods for smallholder producers by way of technical assistance and training on sustainable farming systems, seed banks, water conservation, promotion of traditional and locally adapted crops, helping farmers to get organized in cooperatives as well as organic marketing support. As non-profits, they do not have a commercial or business-oriented approach but focus on long-term sustainable rural development. In addition to promoting sustainable production methods, NGOs started supporting farmers in finding market outlets for their produce in local rural and nearby urban markets. For instance, they facilitate formation of professional, for-profit marketing organizations and value-addition through processing and branding of organic products.

Some of these NGO-driven marketing initiatives are incorporated as producer companies or cooperatives. Their members are mostly small and marginal farmers. While organic cotton grown by these farmers is mostly exported, their food products are distributed in the domestic market through regionally oriented supply chains. The range of value-added and processed products is small, and often the products are not professionally branded. Most of these initiatives operate with a PGS system or are not certified at all. Typical retail channels are small organic stores and direct marketing for instance on farmers' markets or through home delivery. Not all producer cooperatives and farmer-owned companies necessarily engage only in direct marketing as a distribution model. For instance, the producer company Dharani FaM Coop (Timbaktu Organic) sells wholesale and through retailers with a regular retail margin. However, the supply chain is shorter than for conventional products, and shorter than those of branded organic companies that operate through distributors and conventional retail chains.

By reducing the involvement of intermediaries in the value chain, the share of the consumer price that goes directly to the farmer increases while keeping selling prices affordable. The examples of farmer-owned companies we looked at do not sell through organized retail chains. One of the reasons is that these require third-party certification, whereas farmer-producer organizations often work with PGS or are in conversion to organic. Many grassroots organizations also have an explicit Fairtrade policy, guaranteeing participatory processes and a higher share of the profits for farmer members.

While the origin of the organic sector lies in civil society movements, in recent years, a growing number of commercially oriented companies have entered the scene. These are either newly founded companies or existing ones that started shifting their marketing activities from export to the domestic market. Some of these companies have their own production base on company-owned farms, but most of them procure from contract farmers or independent suppliers. These companies concentrate on processing, packaging and branding of organic products. They typically source from large farmers or traders, operate on an India-wide scale, with centralized supply chains, and many also make a significant part of their revenue through export sales. All their organic products are third-party certified and labelled with the India Organic label.

Typical retail channels for the commercial organic sector are company-owned branded organic outlets, supermarkets and, of late, e-commerce operators who sell organic products from different suppliers. Despite its growth, the organized, commercially oriented organic industry is still only a small part of domestic organic trade. The Organic Trade Association remarks that "(t)he packaged organic food industry is highly fragmented, with a large portion of the business accounted for by unorganized players" (OTA 2010: 3).

It is important to note that while most stakeholders fit roughly into either end of the continuum from farmer producer organizations and NGO-supported initiatives on one end to commercial organic companies on the other, not all attributes of a particular venture are necessarily strictly aligned, and there are many examples of mixed forms. For instance, some grassroots organizations use third-party certification in addition to PGS, and supply to retailers that add a high margin. On the other hand, some conventional organized retail chains source directly from farmers.

Table 4-1: Ownership and support structures in the organic production sector [1]

Stakeholders	Mumbai	Bangalore	Hyderabad
Commercial organic companies, processors and brands	9	11	4
Commercial companies founded or supported by NGOs	0	2	0
Producer companies and cooperatives	1	4	4
TOTAL	10	17	8

(1) Numbers do not include companies that sell only in export markets, or only organic cotton.

Table 4-1 shows the range of ownership structures and varying degrees of support from non-profit organizations for marketing organizations in Mumbai,

Bangalore and Hyderabad[13]. The majority of organic companies, processors and brands are incorporated as for-profit private limited companies. In Bangalore, two commercial organic ventures were founded by non-profit foundations and are supported in their outreach work to smallholder producers by these. Some for-profit companies such as Morarka Organic Foods Pvt. Ltd. are associated with a foundation that provides extension services to farmers, while some grassroots NGOs develop marketing activities for small and marginal farmers as a separate branch. The latter often opt for a hybrid model of organization that links a non-profit society, trust or foundation with a for-profit marketing organization (see Chapter 5.2).

Six of the nine producer companies and cooperatives mentioned in Table 3-2 were founded or are supported by externally funded NGOs. For instance, the NGO Centre for Sustainable Agriculture in Hyderabad (see Case Study 6) works with farmer cooperatives in a radius of up to 150 km around Hyderabad. The NGO cooperates with other local NGOs such as CROPS and SERP. Through their work of promoting NPM since 2004, Centre for Sustainable Agriculture and its partner NGOs managed to bring 34 lakh acres across Andhra Pradesh under pesticide-free cultivation (Borah 2012). Part of their activities in recent years has been to help farmers set up a number of cooperative-owned organic food outlets in rural and local small town markets of Andhra Pradesh, to organize deliveries to consumers in Hyderabad and to launch the Sahaja Aharam Organic Consumer Cooperative.

Other initiatives are supported by the government. For instance, in Hyderabad, direct sales of NPM vegetables from farmers in a nearby village are supported by a government programme led by the semi-governmental organization SERP and HACA, and the farmers' federation Jaivik Krishik Society in Bangalore is supported in their marketing activities directly by the Government of Karnataka. Based in Dehradun, the NGO Navdanya procures directly from farmers, manages the processing and branding and sells in their own retail outlets in New Delhi, Dehradun and Mumbai.

When keeping the structure of this continuum and the framework in Figure 4-1 in mind while classifying organic stakeholders, it becomes apparent that the degree of regionalization of supply chains is closely linked to their sustainability. Notably, small-scale and regionally oriented supply chains reduce transport distances, minimize losses and energy use in processing and storage, and

---

13 Note that producer companies are often not registered in the major cities; for instance, Timbaktu Organic is an important supplier to retailers in both in Hyderabad and Bangalore, but not counted here as it is located in Anantapur District.

promote producer and consumer ownership of their food network. By reducing the involvement of intermediaries in the value chain, the financial benefit for smallholder producers increases while keeping retail prices low.

In the following chapters, we present the models of organic food distribution in urban centres that resulted from our empirical work in Mumbai, Bangalore and Hyderabad. Several case studies illustrate the wide variety of distribution models and the overlaps that exist between them wherever organic stakeholders use various marketing channels simultaneously.

4.2 Overview: Organic Retail in Mumbai, Bangalore and Hyderabad

The three cities covered by this study show marked differences in the overall size of the organic sector and in popular retail formats for organic products. The reasons for these variations are a complex play of economic, sociological and historical factors. According to a national retail chain representative, climate plays an important role. While Hyderabad is a good region for growing fruits, Bangalore has a climatic advantage for fruits and vegetables, allowing producers to grow more varieties and larger quantities. In the Mumbai region, farmers are comparatively well educated and have access to sophisticated technologies such as greenhouses. Mumbai is also the biggest consumer market, with a wide range of consumer segments and a cosmopolitan character. Surprisingly, although Mumbai is the largest consumer market of the three cities included in this study, Bangalore has more total organic sales and a greater number of organic food outlets. What sets Bangalore apart especially is its number of organic specialty stores and supermarkets that sell organic food (see Table 4-2 and Appendix 2). Based largely on data from Bangalore, our total market size projections per city are based on the assumption that the average sales value per store is similar in all cities. In the case of Mumbai, our total projection may therefore require some adjustment, as prices there are generally higher.

The India-wide retail chain Fabindia reports maximum sales of organic food in the North region, followed by West, and then the South and East markets put together. This pattern can be attributed to regional differences in food habits, food culture and price-consciousness. By contrast, our data suggest that Bangalore is the largest urban organic market in India. The lower sales figures of this particular chain in Bangalore may in fact be explained by the fact that

Bangaloreans have many other options for buying organic compared to North India.

Table 4-2: Organic market coverage in terms of stakeholders and outlets per city

	Mumbai	*Bangalore*	*Hyderabad*
Total number of organic stakeholders	82	70	41
Organic stakeholders per 100,000 inhabitants	0.44	0.82	0.53
Total number of organic outlets	151	180	93
Organic outlets per 100,000 inhabitants	0.83	2.12	1.21
Total organic market size projection	INR 17.9 crore	INR 21.4 crore	INR 9.9 crore

As Table 4-2 illustrates, Bangalore has the highest organic market coverage of the three cities examined for this study. The total number of stores selling organic food is slightly higher than in Mumbai and twice as high as in Hyderabad. The ratio of organic outlets per one lakh inhabitants is also significantly higher. Hyderabad, with its relatively small number of organic outlets, has a disproportionately high ratio of outlets to inhabitants. This is partly explained by the fact that we counted eight Organic Express outlets in corporate offices and IT parks.

In addition to having the highest density of organic food outlets, Bangalore also has better availability of fresh organic vegetables and, more recently, organic dairy products. These two product categories can serve as indicators of the stage of development and differentiation of a city's organic sector. They are logistically most difficult to procure and – together with processed and value-added products – are among the categories pursued last by organic companies and retailers.

The store count and sales projections for Bangalore are shown in Table 4-3. According to our estimate, the bulk of organic food sales in the city goes through organized retail, most of which are regional or national chains. The second-largest share is held by organic specialty stores, followed closely by non-food stores that sell organic food products, such as Fabindia and Mother Earth. Since reliable data was not accessible for all stakeholders, the figure for organized retail in particular is based largely on our estimates rather than reported sales figures. We made a conservative estimate of both the total number of organized retailers and the average sales value per outlet; therefore this figure is likely to be somewhat higher. Also, while our figures are based on the situation in 2011 and early 2012, rapid developments in the organic food sector suggest that the figures were already significantly higher by the end of 2012, especially for organized retail, organic specialty stores and online retail, which have the highest growth rates. For Hyderabad and Mumbai, we were unable to obtain sufficient sales figures to make a realistic projection of the overall market size. Our estimate – based on average sales figures in Bangalore, scattered data for sales in Mumbai and Hyderabad, and the total number of outlets – is that the market in Bangalore is similar in size to that of Mumbai, and approximately double the size of Hyderabad.

Table 4-3: Bangalore: Estimated sales per distribution channel and total market size projection

Distribution channel[1]	Stake-holders	Outlets	Estimated total sales p.a.	Share of total organic sales
Organic specialty stores	22	23	INR 6,90,00,000	32.2%
Health food stores	0	0	INR 0	0%
Non-food stores	3	17	INR 5,10,00,000	23.8%
Organic and natural bazaars	1	1	INR 2,40,000	0.1%
Direct marketing, CSA	1	1	INR 2,40,000	0.1%
Restaurants, catering	7	7	INR 1,68,00,000	7.8%
Online retail, home delivery	2	n/a	INR 31,20,000	1.4%
Traditional retail, other stores	1	1	INR 2,40,000	0.1%
Organized retail – chains	>13	>120	INR 7,20,00,000	33.7%
Organized retail – standalone	3	3	INR 18,00,000	0.8%
TOTAL	70	180	INR 21,44,40,000	100%

(1) Explanations see Chapters 4.2 to 4.7 and Appendix 2.

Availability of organic food, as well as awareness and demand among consumers, vary widely across different parts of each city. Neighbourhoods with a concentration of SEC A and B households with average monthly household incomes of over 10,000 (Datta 2010) generally have the best availability of organic food. Organized retail stores are located in all parts of the city. Most organized retail chains do not stock organic products in all of their outlets, although some plan to do so in the future. They take stocking decisions based on assumptions regarding demand and local purchasing power of consumers in a specific area, or by trial and error, based on the development of sales over time.

In Mumbai, organic shops are concentrated in South Mumbai and the Western Suburbs. In Hyderabad, Banjara Hills and the surrounding areas have the highest coverage of organic outlets and delivery options. Gachibowli and Tarnaka also have good availability. In Bangalore, availability of organic products is spread more evenly across the city. Concentrations of organic specialty stores are found in many neighbourhoods across the city, for instance in Jayanagar, JP Nagar and Bannerghatta Road in the South, in Rajajinagar, Malleshwaram and Dollars Colony in the North, and Whitefield, Indiranagar and Koramangala in the East.

In the following sections, we look at organic food distribution models in the surveyed cities and assess availability of organic products, the relative importance of different marketing models, and specific strengths and weaknesses of each city's organic sector.

4.3 Organic Specialty Stores, Markets and Health Food Stores

To date, there are very few fully organic stores in India. The Green Path – previously called Era Organics – in Bangalore opened in 2007 and was the first fully certified organic store in India. However, after stocking some products that were PGS labelled but not third-party certified, the store lost its certified status. The Down to Earth store in Mumbai, which is owned by Morarka Organic Foods, sells only certified organic products of their own brand, but is not certified as a store. Since the vast majority of organic stores in India are neither certified nor fully organic, for the purposes of this study, we considered a store an organic specialty store if more than 50% of its food products are organic, taking into account both third-party certified organic and PGS labelled products. By contrast, shops where organic products constitute significantly less than 50% of the total product range were counted in the natural and health food store category. Fully organic supermarket chains, which are increasingly common in mature organic markets such as the USA and Europe, are non-existent in India to date, although a few organic stores have started to develop in that direction by rapidly expanding their product range.

Table 4-4: Organic stores per city by opening year

City	before 2005	2005 - 2009	2009 - 2011	2012	Year unknown
Mumbai	2	1	11	> 8	5
Bangalore	4	4	8	> 2	7
Hyderabad	0	1	5	0	0

While a few pioneer organic stores opened in Mumbai and Bangalore before 2005, the majority of organic specialty stores opened after 2009. Bangalore has the highest number of stores founded before 2009, followed by Mumbai. The first organic store in Hyderabad, 24 Mantra in Banjara Hills (see Case Study 1), opened in 2005. It is the flagship store of Sresta Bioproducts Pvt. Ltd. While the number of organic specialty stores in Hyderabad has grown from one to six in just three years since 2009, it is still small compared to Mumbai and Bangalore. New stores opened in all three cities at an accelerated rate in 2012, but we could not account for all new ones in our survey. Therefore, the count for 2012 is to be read as a minimum number, and the numbers in the "unknown" column represent mostly stores that opened between 2009 and 2011.

The number of organic chain stores is relatively small, with 3 in Mumbai, 1 in Bangalore and none in Hyderabad. Rather than opening more chain stores, Morarka Organic Foods chose to partner with franchise stores – branded stores where 90% of the product range is Morarka's Down to Earth brand. Sresta Bioproducts is planning to follow a similar franchising strategy.

Case Study 1:

24 Mantra: Sresta Bioproducts Pvt. Ltd.

Of all retail outlets selling organic food in Hyderabad, the 24-Letter-Mantra Organic Store (recently renamed into 24 Mantra – The Organic Store) in Banjara Hills has the broadest organic product range. The shop and brand name "24 Mantra" are owned by Sresta Bioproducts Ltd., the company that started the first India-wide organic retail chain in 2005. After initially opening their own branded stores in several cities, the company meanwhile cut back to one flagship store in Hyderabad.

The product range consists of a comprehensive range of grains and pulses, as well as spices, tea, jams, bread, biscuits, snacks and a few ready-to-eat products. Part of the shop is a bistro selling small meals, snacks, biscuits, ice-cream and milkshakes, not all of which are fully organic. The shop also sells a few non-organic products, because currently the full product range is not (yet) available in organic quality. All products in the shop that are not organic are advertised as "natural". Those products that are certified organic correspond to the EU 2092/91, USA NOP and Indian NPOP standards. The National Sales Manager of Sresta Bioproducts estimated in an interview in 2011 that the company's products are currently priced 30-40% higher than non-organic products, and prices are expected to come down further as the product range and volumes increase over the next five years. The long-term goal is a price premium of 10-15% more than non-organic.

Part of the fresh produce sold in the Hyderabad store is sourced from farmers in the region, and part of it is grown on a company-owned farm of 7 acres in Medchal, Rangareddy District, about 30 km north of Hyderabad. Products from the vegetable farm are transported to the store in Hyderabad on a daily basis. For other organic products, Sresta Bioproducts established an India-wide supply chain. Raw materials are sourced from all over the country and transported by road to a processing and packaging unit in Medchal. Processing is as decentralized as possible, with facilities all over India. Packaging, on the other hand, is centralized in Hyderabad because it allows the company to have more control over it.

Sresta Bioproducts works with 12,000 contract farmers and has its own organic projects across the country. Since the company requires certain commitments in terms of scope and reliability, bigger farms or groups of farmers are considered as more viable suppliers. Sresta Bioproducts has more than 30,000 acres under organic cultivation across India. The company currently makes more sales in export than in the domestic market, but domestic demand is growing continuously. In 2009, the monthly turnover of the 24 Mantra store in Banjara Hills was INR 800,000. Sresta Bioproducts also sells in bulk and supplies to a growing number of supermarkets across South India. For the future, the company plans to supply in bulk to company canteens and to open new franchise stores.

The majority of organic specialty stores do not sell exclusively organic products but a mix of products including certified organic, in conversion, PGS (see Chapter 3.3) and uncertified organic as well as products that are considered "natural" or "healthy" for various reasons, for instance because they are free from artificial preservatives and colouring agents. Modern retail chains, as a general rule, stock only certified organic or in-conversion products. Small independent retailers, on the other hand, have the liberty of including products that claim to be organically grown but lack certification. Many stakeholders, especially in the grassroots organic movement, place greater emphasis on personal trust in an individual producer than in the anonymous third-party certification system. A significant number of organic producers and producer groups are not certified. Some of them work with PGS or are planning to do so, while others rely more on long-term producer-retailer relationships that are based on personal trust and a transparent supply chain (cf. Chapters 5.5 and 5.6).

In the past few years, more and more new organic stores, even small ones, started branding their own products. As most of them do not do any processing themselves, they were counted as retailer brands rather than organic companies or processor brands in our survey. Additionally, a few organic store owners have their own farmland where they grow a small number of products that they sell unde<r their own brand or without any packaging label. A few stores that are owned by organic processing companies or producer cooperatives sell mainly their own brand: In 2011, these totalled 3 in Mumbai, 8 in Bangalore and 2 in Hyderabad.

Depending on their size and focus, organic stores have an organic product range anywhere between 50 and 1,000 different products, with an average of 200. In non-food stores, the product range depends very much on the individual outlet. Fabindia, for instance, has a total of 350 products under their brand. Although most Fabindia outlets do not stock this full range, the supply chain is organized in such a way that stores can order any product upon request by a customer.

There are great differences in the structure and reach of organic store supply chains. Branded stores like those owned by Morarka Organic Foods and Sresta Bioproducts have a centralized supply chain and source products from all over India. Independent, multi-brand organic stores have a mix of local, unbranded (and sometimes uncertified) products, local organic brands, and suppliers that operate India-wide. Fabindia has an India-wide supply chain, and does co-branding with major organic processing companies. Some privately-owned organic stores even stock imported organic products, for instance when the quality of Indian products is inadequate, or when a product is unavailable in India – which tends to be the case for luxury and fashionable foods like certified organic olive oil, quinoa, pasta or apple cider vinegar.

In 2011, Entrack Organic Haus Pvt. Ltd. entered the Indian market with a new organic retail chain called Organic Haus. It opened its first store in Ahmedabad and two more in Mumbai and Gurgaon in 2012. The stores sell organic products imported exclusively from Germany and Austria, because the founder believes that the quality of imported products is currently not matched by Indian suppliers. With a modern and spacious store design, Organic Haus targets a segment of consumers ready to pay a premium for products of high quality, prestige and exotic origin that are of marginal relevance to average Indian diets.

Organic stores that are run by NGOs or farmer cooperatives tend to source products regionally in a radius of 150 km, or at the most from the same neighbouring federal states up to 300 km. In addition to running organic stores, these initiatives are also often involved in direct marketing (see Chapter 4.4). Small organic stores often source from such organizations, especially for fresh produce – a major bottleneck in organic supply chains. For instance, several small organic stores and the Good Seeds Organic Bazaar in Hyderabad buy directly from Sahaja Aharam, a producer-consumer cooperative that also runs its own store.

In 2011, fresh organic vegetables were available in 8 stores in Bangalore, 4 in Mumbai and 2 in Hyderabad. In all of these stores, vegetables were only available on certain days of the week, and the range varied seasonally. Only 2 organic stores in Bangalore and 2 in Mumbai had organic dairy products. Apart from organic stores, organic animal products are available in some restaurants, but not in other retail stores, from online retailers or home delivery services.

A few organic stores and health food stores have a range of non-organic imported products such as sweets and breakfast cereals that seem to contrast with the organic and health niche, but nevertheless appear to have an overlapping target audience. In addition to food products, many organic specialty stores have a non-food range comprising natural cosmetics, biodegradable household cleaners and detergents, hand-made and recycled products, organic or hand-made textiles, seeds and inputs for terrace gardening, composters and books.

A few organic specialty stores also have a restaurant or in-store bistro that serves organic products, namely 24 Mantra in Hyderabad, and Lumiere and In the Pink in Bangalore. The Yoga House in Mumbai is primarily a yoga studio, restaurant and café that uses organic ingredients, but it also sells some organic food products. Most organic stores in our study offer home delivery, either free of charge or for a delivery fee. Naturally Yours in Mumbai, for instance, offers free home delivery across Mumbai in order to reach a maximum number of customers. Other organic stores have conditions for delivery such as a minimum order amount, or maximum distance.

Table 4-5: Ownership and support structures in organic retail

Store category	Mumbai	Bangalore	Hyderabad
Privately-owned organic stores including chain stores	13	15	5
Stores owned by NGO-supported organic companies	1	2	0
Stores owned by NGOs, cooperatives or producer companies	1	5	1
TOTAL	15	22	6

Most organic specialty stores are proprietorships, except for the larger non-food chains which are private limited companies. Some organic specialty stores are run by farmer cooperatives or non-profit organizations (see Table 4-5). Examples of the latter are Janodaya Trust and Sahaja Samrudha in Bangalore, Sahaja Aharam in Hyderabad, and Navdanya and Yusuf Meherally Centre (YMC) in Mumbai. The Jaivik Mall in Bangalore, which sells products of the Jaivik Krishik Society farmers' association, is supported by the Government of Karnataka.

Monthly sales of organic speciality stores range from less than INR 1 lakh for recent start-ups and small stores up to INR 12 lakh for long-standing and larger stores. The 16 stores in Bangalore from whom we could obtain data reported average monthly sales of INR 2.5 lakh. Daily footfalls ranged from 3 customers to 55, with an average of 26. The total customer reach including home delivery was between a few hundred to several thousand, although most retailers in our sample were not able to give a reliable estimate for this figure. The retailer margins reported by organic stores and other retail stores ranged from 15% to 25%, with the average being 19.8%. Organic companies, by contrast, reported a range from 15% to as much as 35%, with a higher average of 26.6%. Stores that are operated or supported by an NGO had smaller margins, which largely depend on the store's operational costs. In some cases, these are partly subsidized by the NGO, for instance in the form of free space in an NGO's office building.

As a subcategory of organic specialty retail, some stores do not primarily sell food but specialize in other products that fit broadly into a "green" lifestyle, such as handloom, natural dye, organic and Fairtrade garments, home textiles, handicrafts, furniture, natural cosmetics and ayurvedic health products. Among these shops are some chains, notably Fabindia (see Case Study 2) – a pioneer in organic specialty retail and one of the country's most well-known organic brands. Fabindia operates in all three cities covered by this study, with 14 outlets in Mumbai, 14 in Bangalore and 6 in Hyderabad, most of which also sell organic food products. Fabindia is often associated with an organic lifestyle even by consumers who may not be aware of any other organic stores. Another example is Mother Earth, which operates stores in Bangalore and Mumbai, although only two of the stores in Bangalore sold organic food products in 2012. Three other non-food stores in Mumbai sell a small range of organic food products. Two of them are specialty stores for arts, crafts and home deco, and one is a pharmacy chain that has organic products in a few selected outlets. One bookstore in Bangalore and two clothing stores in Hyderabad sell organic food products. One of them is the handloom store Daaram which stocks products from Timbaktu Organic (see Case Study 5) as part of the store's mission to support the marketing activities of small independent village industries, such as handloom fabrics and organic food products.

Case Study 2:

Fabindia Pvt. Ltd.

Fabindia was founded in 1960, primarily as an export house for handloom textiles (Singh 2011). Over the years, the company expanded its presence all over India as well as internationally, with currently 146 stores in India. All Fabindia products are at least partly handmade, and an important component of the company profile is their support for rural artisans. The unique selling points of Fabindia are high product quality combined with a unique ethnic style, store decor and ambience. Garments are of a consciously timeless style so that they can be worn for a long time. Fabindia's declared objective is "to offer customers a complete organic lifestyle" (cited in Carroll 2005). To this end, the company added a small organic food product line to their domestic retail activities in 2004. Since then, the organic food section has grown to 350 products and almost 10% of total domestic sales. The annual growth of organic food sales has slowed down from an initial 100-300% to 45%, but is still significant.

In addition to staple cereals and pulses, Fabindia's food range comprises many value-added and niche products such as muesli, pasta, jams, fruit concentrates, spices and tea. Efforts are being made to expand the range further, as the organic food market is seen as one of the major opportunities for future development (Kalita et al. 2008: 6). Fabindia does not process products but co-brands them with organic companies like Conscious Food, Morarka Organic Foods and others. Not all food products sold at Fabindia are certified organic. The company follows a three-tier internal classification model of certified organic, in conversion and natural (cf. Chapter 3.3). Currently, 60% of Fabindia's food products are certified organic, with the long-term target of offering a fully organic range. A major constraint is the lack of consistency and quality in organic supply as well as cost and bureaucratic requirements of certification for suppliers. For uncertified products, Fabindia commissions laboratory tests to guarantee that products are free from pesticide residues.

All Fabindia stores in India are company-owned, and a franchise model is used for the international market. The majority of domestic sales occur in India's North region, and accordingly Fabindia's main distribution centres are located in Delhi and Jaipur. In addition, products are sourced and dispatched from various places across India.

Fabindia does not have its own storage and processing facilities. Although the company would like to source from farmers directly, in order to support rural producers while keeping the end prices low, this is difficult because at the farm level, products are in a raw state. Processing, packaging and branding is therefore done by organic companies, NGOs and farmer groups on behalf of Fabindia. According to Kalita et al. (2008), Fabindia's sourcing strategy is heavily supplier-centric and follows a centralized hub model of supply chain management. This model apparently causes some problems with long delays in the supply, so that not all organic food products are always available. More recently, Fabindia also started online retail for their entire food range and delivers across India. With regard to advertising, Fabindia relies mainly on word of mouth. It does not have a customer acquisition strategy but focuses mainly on customer retention. Accordingly, about 85% of customers are repeat customers (Kalita et al. 2008). Fabindia uses in-store posters and leaflets to publicize the company's philosophy, the stories behind its products and information on organic farming.

Organic specialty retail also takes place at a number of markets and festivals. Distinct from farmers' markets, which are a form of direct marketing (see Chapter 4.4), this subcategory includes events such as the Nature Bazaar in Mumbai, which started in January 2012 and happens on an irregular basis; organic festivals organized occasionally in Hyderabad by various local NGOs and stakeholders in the organic sector; and fairs and flea markets like Second to None in Bangalore. Hyderabad's first monthly organic market, the Organic Bazaar, was started in January 2012 by the organic start-up Good Seeds. The bazaar is currently not a farmers' market in the strict sense, but rather a forum for various retailers selling organic food products, homemade organic snacks, natural cosmetics and recycled products. Food products are sourced from Sahaja Aharam and various other organic farmers and companies. Organic markets typically also host educational activities on themes like organic agriculture, waste management and other environmental issues. The Farmers' Market in Mumbai is primarily a direct marketing outlet where farmers personally sell their produce. In addition to the farmers, it comprises some stalls that are run by companies and NGOs selling organic food items, handicrafts and other eco-friendly products.

In this study, shops where organic products make up less than 50% of the total product range were classified as natural and health food stores. Many of these stores use words such as green, natural or health in their store name, rather than the word "organic," although some stores that have organic in their name do not necessarily sell mainly organic products. Natural and health food stores are typically small, proprietor-managed and specialize in a variety of items for a healthy lifestyle such as organic products, low-calorie and sugar-free snack items, food supplements, ayurvedic medicines and non-food items like yoga mats, sprouting containers and books. In Mumbai there are 3 such health stores, 2 in Hyderabad, and none in Bangalore. For instance, The Heath Shop in Mumbai is a specialty store for low-calorie snacks and sweets, and it has a sizeable organic range.

The small store Vijaya Enterprises in Hyderabad is another example of a shop catering to health-conscious consumers looking for high-quality health food and other health products. Mostly a non-organic store, it also stocks organic brown rice, wheat, millets, pulses, jaggery, and sometimes vegetables and leafy vegetables. Rice is sourced from small organic farmers in villages around Zaheerabad. According to the shop owner, the non-organic products he sells are grown by small farmers whom he knows personally and who use "very little" chemical inputs. The owner of the store claims to run the business for more than commercial interest; he intends to spread awareness of healthy food and "help the people" by providing healthy food at reasonable prices. Customers come from various socio-economic backgrounds. Some of them travel considerable distances to the store, including from outside Hyderabad. Only about 10% of the customers are aware that some of the products in the store are organic, and according to the owner nobody enquires about organic products. The organic products at Vijaya Enterprises sell at around 20% more than non-organic, but according to the owner those customers who come specifically in order to buy organic products do not mind the higher prices.

4.4 Direct Marketing and Community-Supported Agriculture

Farmer-to-consumer direct marketing refers to a distribution model wherein producers sell directly to consumers, without involving any profit-seeking intermediaries. In Europe, common direct sales formats are farmers' markets and farm shops or stalls. While the bulk of conventional fresh produce in India is sold through markets and roadside stalls, these do not sell any organic produce, and dedicated organic farmers' markets are rare. Farm shops are not common at all due to the larger distances between urban centres and rural production areas combined with difficult transport infrastructure and bad road conditions, small size of farms which does not permit for farm sales infrastructure, and a lack of interest in getting involved in direct sales on the part of many farmers. In India, emerging organic direct marketing channels are farmers' markets and stalls, mobile sales points, home delivery and community-supported agriculture schemes. Direct marketing is typically done by individual farmers as well as cooperatives, producer companies and NGO-supported marketing initiatives. Increasingly, these organizations also supply to commercial retailers in addition to direct marketing. For instance, products from Timbaktu Organic, Sahaja Aharam and Sahaja Samrudha are available at a growing number of organic stores and online retailers.

In many cases, it is actually more appropriate to speak of facilitated direct marketing, because many direct marketing models do involve some kind of intermediary facilitating the marketing activities on a non-profit basis. This could be either an associated NGO or a producer-owned marketing company. Many direct marketing initiatives – whether cooperatives, producer companies or community-supported agriculture – were launched by a non-profit rural development NGO. These NGOs started facilitating the marketing activities of member farmers or associated farmers as an extension of their rural development and sustainable agriculture programmes (cf. Chapter 4.1). Over the years of their operations in rural areas, these NGOs realized that the growing number of farmers who shift to sustainable farming practices also require market access for their high-value organic produce. In the long run, the target is to scale up and professionalize marketing operations to a point where they become financially self-supporting. Overheads and salaries of the NGO staff are often externally funded, so the full benefit of the organic premium that consumers pay goes directly to the farmers.

The actual sales, for instance at bazaars and roadside stalls, are mostly not done by farmers themselves. They lack the required time and capabilities, and logistic constraints make it difficult for them to reach consumers in the city directly. Therefore, farmers often delegate the sales activities to an affiliated NGO. For instance, Centre for Sustainable Agriculture in Hyderabad experimented with an organic farmers market held at the NGOs office in Hyderabad, but soon found that sales volumes did not justify the time and effort that it took the famers to come to the city regularly. Similarly, the (non-organic) Rythu Bazaars, which were set up by the Government of Andhra Pradesh in 1999 as farmers' markets to give producers an opportunity to sell directly to consumers at affordable rates, have come under criticism because professional traders and vendors largely took over the vending activities. Nevertheless, even in those cases of facilitated direct marketing where farmers do not do the selling in person, the link between producers and consumers becomes a lot shorter, more participatory and more equitable than in conventional supply chains that involve profit-seeking intermediaries.

One of the few examples where farmers personally sell to and interact with consumers on a regular basis is the Farmers' Market in Mumbai (see Case Study 3). It was started in 2010 as Mumbai's first ever exclusively organic farmers' market with the vision of making fresh organic vegetables readily available to urban consumers, and thus motivating more people to consume organic food. Until recently, only staples and dry provisions were available in organic quality in urban markets. Organic vegetables, fresh from the farm, are high in demand by consumers (cf. Rao et al. 2006), but are much more difficult to find. The Farmers's Market also aims to support organic producers by paying a fair price and to raise awareness among urban consumers of the need of farmers to earn a decent livelihood. In addition to farmers selling fresh produce, a variety of other companies sell organic and natural products as well as organic meals and snacks. The costs incurred for renting the market space are born by the fees for these stalls and by stall sponsors. The farmers get to use the space free of charge and benefit from receiving an organic premium directly from consumers.

Case Study 3:

"No Bargaining": The Farmers' Market in Mumbai

The Farmers' Market in Mumbai was initiated by Kavita Mukhi, founder of the organic company Conscious Food and an early pioneer of Mumbai's organic movement. Kavita Mukhi started the market in March 2010 with a small number of farmers from rural areas beyond Nashik, approximately 300 km from Mumbai. By 2011, the market hosted 12 to 15 farmers selling the produce grown by 20 associated farmers. Their stalls feature mostly vegetables, some fruits and occasionally other items like jaggery. Apart from the farmers, a number of other vendors sell organic coffee and tea, meals, snacks and sweets, packaged organic food, and non-food items like natural cosmetics, organic cotton T-shirts, accessories and handicrafts.

The market is organized every Sunday during the dry seasons because vegetable supply is irregular during the monsoon. Initially, the market was held on a municipal grounds, which was advantageous due to affordable rent. After a very successful start, however, there were some disagreements with the local authorities, so the market shifted to a private playschool ground on a popular commercial street in Bandra West. The new venue was much smaller, and the rent higher. While farmers get stall space free of charge, other exhibitors have to pay a fee. These stall fees can be an obstacle for some organizations who would like to participate in the market, but are necessary to recover the rent for the venue and allow farmers to participate free of cost. In their advertising on Facebook and on leaflets, the Farmers' Market calls upon the public to sponsor stalls for the farmers. As the organizer, Kavita Mukhi does not get involved directly with the sales that the farmers make; she sees her role as limited to providing the venue and helping the farmers get a fair price.

At this stage, the target audience for the Farmers' Market is intended to be upper middle class. The organizers believe that this section of society can afford to pay a higher premium to support farmers who do not receive government subsidies for organic production. Since 2011, the market occasionally takes place at the Mahalaxmi Race Course in South Mumbai, where a lot more space is available. In addition to the regular stalls that sell organic produce, a greater number of additional stalls sell snacks, packaged organic products and non-food products. Live music in the evening and the overall atmosphere at the race course turn these markets into a leisurely shopping experience and a festive event. In general, part of the success of the market is owed to its atmosphere. While some people go early in the morning or send their servants to buy produce, others take their whole families for an outing. The latter spend time looking at all the stalls, eating snacks and talking with vendors and other customers. In 2012, the market shifted from Bandra to two new locations in Andheri and Maharashtra Nature Park.

Apart from the long distance and difficult transport logistics, the greatest challenge for the farmers is the extra time required for participating in the market. Packing, transport, the actual market and the journey back takes farmers away from their farms for three whole days. Nevertheless, this effort is worthwhile: The Farmers' Market gives producers an assured and profitable sales opportunity, enabling them to grow higher-value crops like fruits and vegetables in addition to non-perishables like grains, pulses and sugarcane. Growing fresh produce increases their labour input, but it has also improved their revenue significantly. The farmers benefit from the fixed prices at the market – a large sign behind the vegetable stalls says "No Bargaining: Organic is Priceless" – because it gives them an assured income that is independent from the price fluctuations in the conventional market. When the market first started, some customers did attempt to bargain, but they quickly accepted the fixed prices, which at times can be even lower than regular market prices and thus to the advantage of consumers. Mostly, participating farmers manage to sell all produce by Sunday afternoon.

The main mission of the Farmers' Market is to give farmers an opportunity to build a viable and sustainable livelihood. Kavita Mukhi's hope is that "people support the market, understand and value the farmers' work and what it means to the larger community, society itself" (quoted in Datt 2010). It is also a platform for educating customers about organic agriculture and raising awareness of the dangers of pesticides, and of environmental issues more generally. One of the mottos of the market is "Bring your kids & your carry bags"; customers appreciate this philosophy, and most of them cooperate readily. Some exhibitors distribute leaflets and brochures, and there are occasional documentary screenings and discussions. The certification agency Ecocert also sponsors a stall and gives information about organic certification to visitors. For Kavita Mukhi, one major challenge with regard to consumers lies in making people aware of the dangers of pesticides used in non-organic agriculture. She wants people to change their priorities, and to spend more on quality food.

In addition to economic benefits for farmers and fresh organic produce for consumers, the market provides a venue for personal interaction which both farmers and consumers appreciate. Consumers find in the Farmers' Market a space where they can meet and connect with likeminded people. The market has a customer base of 200 to 300 people every Sunday in 2011. Part of its success can be attributed to proactive public relations: For example, a Facebook group and mailing list appeal to a young, cosmopolitan target group with high health awareness and purchasing power. Overall, visitors are a mixed group with a concentration on upper class, educated and highly aware consumers.

All the farmers selling vegetables at the market are certified organic, but some of the other products sold at the market, such as meals and snacks, are not necessarily certified. In cases where they are not, Kavita Mukhi says she makes "very sure" that she knows the people and their background personally, and has seen their farms and organic production methods. This pragmatism is necessary in light of the fact that organic is still a small niche market in the city, and organic supplies for many products are limited or unavailable. The success of the market is based on personal trust together with Kavita Mukhi's extensive network in Mumbai's organic sector, her reputation among urban consumers as the founder of a reputable organic brand, and the enthusiasm and personal commitment she invested.

The case of the Farmers' Market demonstrates that incentives have to be provided to make travelling to the city worth the farmers' while: They are willing to travel over 300 km every Sunday because the market gives them much better returns compared to selling their produce at conventional rates in the local markets, and because the market provides a venue for personal interaction and building a community rather than selling to anonymous consumers.

An initiative of the Hyderabad Agricultural Cooperative Association (HACA) together with Society for Elimination of Rural Poverty (SERP) found another solution to direct marketing: One member of a farmer group travels to Hyderabad on four days a week, selling vegetables grown on non-pesticide management (NPM[14]) farms on behalf of the entire group of farmers. This enables the other members of the group to focus on core farming activities. This strategy is a good option where one farmer has a larger farm size so that

---

14 Definition see Chapter 3.1.

they are able to employ farm labour for day-to-day farm work. Part of SERP's mission is to link producers in peri-urban areas to urban middle-class consumers, thereby enabling producer access to new marketing channels. HACA facilitates sales by providing a stall space in their building free of charge for the farmers. This kind of subsidy is crucial for making the operation financially viable. Initially, vegetables from Manchal village, located 50 km from Hyderabad, were sold at the HACA office building in a central area of Hyderabad once a week. Since 2008, sales were expanded to four days a week, and the regular customer base grew to 100-125 per day. While the vegetables are not certified organic, independent laboratory tests verify that they do not contain any pesticide residues. Many consumers who buy at the HACA stall are not even aware of NPM or organic farming; their major incentives are farm-fresh vegetables, convenient location near residential and office buildings, and the affordable prices. Despite subsidies for non-organic production that distort production costs and prices, the NPM vegetables are hardly more expensive.

The farmer association Deccan Development Society (DDS) developed an innovative model for mobile sales that is very popular with a small but dedicated group of consumers spread across Hyderabad. On two days a week, their mobile sales van – called Organic Mobile – tours several neighbourhoods in Hyderabad and reaches 50-100 consumers regularly. Based in Zaheerabad in Western Andhra Pradesh, DDS has worked with small farmers in Medak District since 1983. Their main mission is to promote sustainable farming methods and to revive the traditional regional food culture which is based on millets and pulses. DDS promotes agro-biodiversity through developing village-level seed banks and cultivation of millets as traditional, highly nutritious and agro-climatically well adapted crops that are ideally suited for rainfed organic farming in the arid regions of the Deccan Plateau. In order to create a market for small and marginal farmers who grow millets and pulses organically, DDS developed a brand and product packaging, labelled with the PGS Organic India logo (see Chapter 3.3), and started selling those products to consumers in Zaheerabad and Hyderabad. In addition to supporting organic production and marketing, DDS raises awareness of nutritional qualities of millets and promotes traditional recipes collected from farming women in order to promote consumption of millets and pulses.[15]

The Sahaja Samrudha Organic Producers Company Ltd. in Bangalore sells about half of its volumes through bulk, and half through retail. In addition to a

---

15 See informational brochure on http://milletindia.org/EatSmart-EatMillets.pdf, and MINI et al. (2008).

store in the organization's warehouse and office, the farmer-owned company sells at a stall inside the WIPRO campus, and since 2011 through home delivery to a small number of households. In Hyderabad, the farmer-owned company Chetna Organic Agriculture Producer Company Ltd. (COAPCL) exports organic and Fairtrade cotton and also sells organic food products wholesale to processors.

When Centre for Sustainable Agriculture in Hyderabad found that it was not feasible for farmers to come to Hyderabad for selling their produce directly to consumers on a regular basis, the NGO developed a different model of facilitated direct marketing that combines several distribution channels: bulk supplies to retailers and catering businesses; a small organic store on the premises of Centre for Sustainable Agriculture; and delivery to pick-up points across the city where members of the Sahaja Aharam Organic Consumer Cooperative collect their weekly organic food basket.

Consumer cooperatives like Sahaja Aharam can be seen as part of the community-supported agriculture movement. This term was first used for consumer-producer alliances in Japan, the US and Europe (see Info Box). In India's agriculture sector, there is a strong tradition of cooperative forms of organization. Traditionally, informal supply relationships have existed between a particular farmer or vendor that regularly sold to the same consumers in a neighbourhood, for instance through door-to-door delivery of fresh leafy vegetables. In these systems, the farmer had an assured income from a committed customer base, and the customers could rely on a fresh and convenient daily supply of seasonal produce. More than a mere exchange of goods, these long-term relationships also provided a site for social interactions and were a source of information for consumers, for instance for recipes and advice on which vegetables are best in a particular season. Though not formalized or documented, these informal contracts implied a high degree of commitment, reliability and stability over time.

In modern urban settings, these traditional informal contractual relationships have started to break down gradually. Newly emerging initiatives are now trying to fill the remaining gap by enabling farmer-consumer interactions at markets or by forming formal alliances between groups of consumers and organic producers in the form of community-supported agriculture. While tie-ups between individual farmers and urban consumers have existed for a long time, formalized community-supported agriculture initiatives are being formed only in recent years as part of the localized organic farming movement.

Info Box:
Community-Supported Agriculture (CSA)

Community-supported agriculture is a model of direct marketing that aims to build long-term relationships between groups of producers and groups of urban consumers. Examples from other parts of the world are the teikei ("partnership") system in Japan and community initiatives in Switzerland that emerged in the 1970s. From there, the CSA movement spread to the USA and eventually to other European countries[16].

CSA is a highly adaptive model that takes different forms different local contexts. The action manual "A Share in the Harvest" published by the Soil Association – the principal organization promoting the CSA concept in the UK – defines CSA as "a partnership between farmers and consumers where the responsibilities and rewards of farming are shared. (...) CSA is a shared commitment to building a more local and equitable agricultural system, one that allows farmers to focus on good farming practices and still maintain productive and profitable farms." (Soil Association 2009: 3) This definition emphasizes one of the key characteristics shared by CSAs around the world: the sharing of risks and benefits between producers and consumers. Consumers take on a greater responsibility than in conventional marketing systems, for example by holding a farm share, prepaying an entire season, or becoming members of a consumer cooperative and giving farmers a purchasing guarantee. CSAs are often organized as cooperatives or cooperative associations. All CSAs have some form of face-to-face contact between producers and consumers, for instance when produce is exchanged, at occasional farm visits, or when consumers work as volunteers for the CSA. Typically, the farms involved in CSA models are small and medium size family farms that work with organic or bio-dynamic farming systems. Exchange of produce can happen through farm shops or markets, at pick-up points, or through box delivery schemes.

CSA was found by several authors to make positive contributions to sustainable development (Kneafsey et al. 2008; Seyfang 2009; Kloppenburg et al. 2000; Lass et al. 2001). The benefits include localized supply chains that help reduce food miles and keep money circulating in the local economy; sustainable farming practices that require less energy input and conserve water and soils; reduced packaging; more diverse and economically viable farms; generating employment and at the same time making organic produce available

---

16 See Henderson (2010) for an overview of the global history of CSA.

to broader socioeconomic strata at affordable price levels; and strengthening local communities and fostering values of participation and reconnection of producers, consumers and food.

CSA is today a globally growing movement. Its growth is at least partly a response to food scandals and hazards such as pesticide residues, and to an increasingly industrialized and globalized food system that "fails to provide adequate nourishment for large numbers of people, does not account for many environmental costs, and concentrates decisions over food in fewer and fewer hands" (Henderson 2007: 11).

In India, community-supported agriculture initiatives emerged in different cities over the past few years. While these initiatives are highly diverse and adapted to local contexts, they also share many key characteristics with CSAs around the world. Like in other countries, CSAs in India emerged from the grassroots organic movement and are based on sustainable farming systems. In most community-supported agriculture initiatives in India, an organization such as an NGO or a consumer cooperative plays a facilitating role on a non-profit basis to help institutionalize the relationship between producers and consumers and organize the marketing activities.

CSAs in India do not usually work with third-party certification but emphasize personal relationships, trust and transparency as more important. Some work with PGS to guarantee sustainable production standards. Most of these initiatives are incorporated as cooperatives, cooperative associations or registered societies. The starting point of the CSA initiatives we looked at for this study was either a group of urban consumers with an educated background who are keen to procure fresh organic vegetables or a rural development NGO. Their mission is to provide wholesome food to consumers, and to make a good, dignified life possible for producers and consumers by circumventing the established market structures. Consumer members of CSA schemes are motivated by a variety of factors which include health and environmental benefits of organic food, a concern for farmers' wellbeing and political issues surrounding rural development and the agrarian crisis. They also share a desire to localize food supply, strengthen local food sovereignty and reconnect to the sources of food and the people producing it. The CSA marketing system is not just a relationship of buying and selling; it is as much about personal interaction and exchange, about redefining the farmer-consumer relationship and bring consumers closer to the farms and farmers.

While farmer's markets, stalls and home delivery essentially maintain a clear seller-customer relationship, CSA goes beyond this to engage consumers and producers in a long-term partnership. The degree to which consumers are actively involved in the marketing model varies between different initiatives. Within the CSA category, our survey suggested that it makes sense in the Indian context to distinguish between two basic models:

- CSAs which involve a consumer-producer partnership in the form of prepaid subscriptions to a privately-owned or NGO-run marketing company; an example is GORUS in Pune (see Case Study 4)

- CSAs with a higher level of participatory involvement and long-term commitment of consumers, for instance in the form of membership in a registered society or a farm share; examples are Sahaja Aharam in Hyderabad (see Case Study 6), MOFCA in Mumbai (see Case Study 8) and Econet in Bangalore

In initiatives of the second category, most of the administrative and some of the logistic work is done by volunteers. Customers of GORUS in Pune, by contrast, do not contribute any volunteer work. It is all the more important in their case to build long-term customer loyalty through personal interactions during farm visits. CSA groups give consumers a platform for connecting with each other, making new contacts with likeminded people and establishing a sense of community in a mostly anonymous urban context. While some organizations, for example Hari Bhari Tokri in Mumbai, supply a mixed basket of whatever vegetables are seasonally available, others give the option of ordering quantities and varieties for each delivery. Subscribers of GORUS get a chance to order individual products and quantities every week. The list of what is available is edited every week and adapted to seasonal availability. While this requires meticulous production planning, weekly adaptations of the online order form and a lot more labour for packing the personalized crates, experiments showed that most households in Pune much prefer being able to choose their vegetable varieties.

Case Study 4:

„Organic Veggies in my Inbox": GORUS in Pune

Although the following case study is located in Pune, Maharashtra, and not in one of the three primary cities that this study examines, it was included here for two major reasons: Firstly, there are few examples of formalized community-supported agriculture initiatives in India to date, and GORUS has demonstrated how such a concept with origins abroad can be adapted to the urban Indian context. Secondly, and more generally, it serves as an example of how a functional peri-urban organic vegetable supply chain can be set up on a small scale. The case study provides a number of insights and important lessons both specifically for other community-driven organic initiatives and generally for stakeholders trying to set up organic supply chains in India in general. Creating supply chains for perishable produce currently presents a major challenge to organic food marketing in urban markets of India.

GORUS[17], or Gomukh Centre for Rural Sustainability, is a community-supported agriculture that was started as a pilot project by Gomukh Environmental Trust for Sustainable Development. For more than fifteen years, this NGO has worked with small farmers in the Pune region on sustainable rural development and integrated watershed development. In 2008, GORUS started growing a variety of vegetables organically on a small plot of land at the Gomukh Trust's farm, located 45 km from Pune. Initially, the produce was sold to a small number of households in Pune, but by 2011, 25 farmers became involved and the customer base grew to 150 households.

In order to organize their supply chain efficiently, GORUS makes use of latest technology: Customers order their weekly deliveries through an online form that contains a list of 35-40 vegetables and other organic groceries. Once orders are placed, the GORUS coordinators send a message to each farmer via mobile phone, specifying the exact quantities they should harvest. The farmers bring this produce to the collection centre, where the individual boxes are packed. In combination with the small scale and regional focus, this system of harvesting only what is ordered and delivering it within 36 hours allows farmers to minimize wastage and risks. Any produce that is left over gets dried or processed into powder and puree, using adapted small-scale technology, such as solar driers and manual pulping machines, in order to promote value-addition on the village level.

On three days a week, a total of 600 to 700 kg of organically grown vegetables is distributed across different parts of Pune by the GORUS truck. Upon delivery, customers are requested to sign a delivery register. GORUS has implemented a prepaid system in which customers make an advance payment

---

17 "Organic veggies in my inbox" is the title of a newspaper article published about GORUS (Dharmadhikary 2010).

of INR 2,000 from which their weekly purchases are deducted. One of the challenges for GORUS is the fact that some consumers do not settle their bills on time and owe money, even though the project has little working capital and needs to pay the farmers regularly.

Ashwin Paranjpe, initiator and coordinator of GORUS, had previous experience with community-supported agriculture in the USA and in Spain. He emphasizes that he considers GORUS's activities to be decidedly different from a typical certified organic marketing model. It is not just a relationship of buying and selling; in addition to supplying fresh, local and seasonal organic produce, the aim is to promote personal interaction and exchange, to redefine the farmer-consumer relationship and bring consumers closer to the farm and farmers. To this end, GORUS arranges farm visits for participating consumers on three weekends a year. In 2011, 150 to 200 people from Pune joined each of these farm visits, many of them with their families. Both farmers and consumers enjoy the personal interaction, which also helps to build long-term customer loyalty, educate consumer about principles of organic agriculture, and raise awareness of broader issues such as rural livelihood conditions, environment and health.

The farmers involved with GORUS have an average landholding of 2-3 acres of which 1/4 acre is cultivated as vegetables. GORUS encourages farmers to have a highly diversified farm system with crops that can be marketed well in the city. With the income they have already made from the vegetable marketing activity, some farmers are now able to set up small greenhouses and thus expand the growing season. For the farmers, the most important advantages of selling through GORUS are an assured market for their produce and avoiding the risks of price fluctuations. They are paid the same rate per kg for every vegetable throughout the year and receive a share of at least 50% of what the consumer pays. Salaries for labourers are also above the local average. This Fairtrade model has worked so far without any legal bond or contract with the farmers, who are officially considered suppliers. Since Gomukh Trust has worked in the area for a long time, their verbal guarantee has been sufficient. In fact, it was their good reputation in the region that helped win the farmers' trust in the first place.

Gomukh Trust initially facilitated the project by co-funding staff salaries and providing land, capital and infrastructure facilities. Since 2011, marketing activities are financially independent of the NGO and run as a commercial venture with a social focus. Ashwin Paranjpe hopes that in another five years, all infrastructure costs will be fully covered by the vegetable marketing. The project's base of farmers and consumers has grown steadily. While there is already a waiting list of interested consumers, GORUS's rate of expansion has been deliberately slow so as to give farmers time to expand their production gradually. The target capacity is a maximum of 200 families and 50 farmers, a scale at which the project can maintain its basic principles of regional focus, environmental sustainability, and Fairtrade relationships.

4.5 Restaurants and Catering

There are very few organic specialty restaurants in India to date. Most of the ones that do exist are not fully organic but serve food "made with organically grown ingredients, as far as possible," due to the poor availability of a wide range of organic products. In the cities we looked at in this study, Bangalore has the highest number of restaurants and catering businesses that use organic ingredients, followed by Mumbai and then, after a large gap, Hyderabad. The data in Appendix 2 indicates that in 2011, Hyderabad had the highest number of outlets serving ready-to-eat food prepared with organic ingredients. However, out of the total 11 outlets in Hyderabad, as many as 8 are operated by the caterer Organic Express in corporate campuses and IT parks, mostly in Hitec City. They were cut back to 2 during 2012, because the other 6 were not feasible. The number of full-fledged restaurants or bistros serving organic food, or food made with organic ingredients, is much smaller in Hyderabad. Bangalore had 6 restaurants in 2011 that used partly or entirely organic ingredients. One of the larger ones, Lumiere, combines a restaurant with an organic retail store and online retail. The Green Path, also in Bangalore, is not only an organic store, but also a hotel that operates on ecological principles, including an organic slow-food restaurant for hotel guests. Additionally, the eco-resort Our Native Village, located 20 km outside of Bangalore, has its own organic farm and vegan restaurant.

Most restaurants, bistros and cafés that serve organic food are standalone outlets. The only catering chain in the cities covered by this study is Organic Express, an innovative organic start-up operating in Hyderabad and Gurgaon. Organic Express started tapping a niche market in 2009: A large number of young tech professionals usually eat at least one meal per day in the office canteens of IT parks and corporate campuses or at nearby eateries. However, despite growing demand, these office environments lack healthy lunch and snack options. In order to fill this gap, Organic Express offers meals and snacks made with fresh vegetables, millets and unpolished rice, using organically grown ingredients as much as possible, as well as native chicken varieties[18]. Their snack items also cater to the demand for Western and non-traditional food products such as sandwiches.

In Hyderabad, the 24 Mantra flagship store of Sresta Bioproducts has a bistro that serves organic meals, snacks, natural ice-cream and juices. Other than that, only two restaurants in Hyderabad use some organic ingredients. The Hyderabad-based Deccan Development Society runs an organic health food restaurant called Café Ethnic in Zaheerabad, Western Andhra Pradesh. In Mumbai, the traditional thali restaurant Revival Indian Thali uses organic ingredients for selected items on the menu every day. While we are not aware of any fully organic restaurants in Mumbai, there are three organic meal delivery services that use partly or exclusively organic ingredients, each with a different concept. Soulfood uses macrobiotic cooking principles and delivers lunches to households, and Vegan Bites focuses on plant-based, healthy food for delivery and event catering. These meal services use the long-established dabbawala system for delivery, which is affordable, efficient and reliable. The Farmers' Market in Mumbai provides a sales channel for small-scale food enterprises such as Sahi Tiffin, a fully organic catering provider, and several vendors of home-made cakes and desserts that sell to customers directly through delivery or pick-up.

Some restaurants, such as Lumiere and The Green Path in Bangalore, produce some of their organic ingredients on their own farms, but are not entirely self-sufficient. Restaurants and caterers have a wide range of organic suppliers, from small local farms and NGO initiatives that are not necessarily certified organic to larger organic companies. While some restaurants get deliveries directly from suppliers, others also buy from organic specialty stores. This mix of sourcing strategies means that supply chains are both local and national in reach. Ownership of restaurants and catering businesses ranges from proprietorships to NGOs. While some restaurants were established several years ago, there has been a wave of new start-ups during the last few years, especially since 2008.

4.6 Online Retail and Home Delivery Services

In the past two years, several organic online retailers and delivery services were founded that do not have any physical retail outlets. In India, e-commerce is an

---

18 Often referred to as "country chicken," as opposed to industrially raised chickens.

emerging sector which has started to expand only recently. Currently, there are 3 organic enterprises in Mumbai – JiyoOrganic, NaturalMantra and NaturalKart – that sell exclusively online, and two in Bangalore – Organic Impulse and Dubden Green. In addition, a growing number of retailers, from small stores to chains like Fabindia, are adding an online order option to their retail outlets. In Hyderabad, Jiva Organics launched a delivery service in 2012 that takes orders through email and phone. In most of these cases, online ordering is an extension of an existing home delivery model, and customer contact in person and over the phone remains important.

Some organic shops make the bulk of their retail sales through home delivery. For instance, Adi Naturals in Bangalore has been successfully using online ordering systems alongside a physical retail outlet and traditional home delivery for several years. A few organic companies also offer a direct-to-home order option for end consumers, through online or phone orders. This could be a major area of sales expansion in the future; however, to date, specialty retailers have an advantage because their product range tends to be more varied. Following the trend in conventional supermarkets (see Chapter 4.7), some conventional online grocery stores also started including organic products in their product range. For instance, Town Essentials is a mostly conventional online food retailer that has a small range of organic and natural food products and delivers within Bangalore.

Organic online retailers typically offer a few hundred different food products. While some only sell certified and branded organic products, others include non-certified organic products and products marketed as "natural". In addition to organic food, some online stores primarily sell products for a sustainable lifestyle such as natural cosmetics, eco-friendly cleaners or ayurvedic medicines and food supplements. For food products, some retailers stick to local organic suppliers and Indian brands, while others cover a wide range of products from imports such as pasta or quinoa to major Indian organic brands to small local enterprises that use organic ingredients.

At present, only a few online retailers and delivery services are able to offer fresh fruits and vegetables due to supply limitations and logistic difficulties such as inadequate transport infrastructure and lack of cold storage. In Mumbai, JiyoOrganic had over 200 different organic food products in 2011, plus a wide variety of fruits and vegetables, and was planning to add dairy products. Some organic retailers offer delivery of a mixed box of seasonal vegetables, depending on weekly availability. Different from direct marketing and community-supported agriculture (see Chapter 4.4), these delivery services involve an intermediary with a commercial interest in the supply chain between producers and consumers. They also do not require any pre-payment or long-term commitment on the customers' part. While consumers have to pay more for this delivery service, they benefit from a wider product range, professional management and greater reliability than in some non-commercial community-supported agriculture delivery schemes.

Two of the online retailers in Mumbai deliver India-wide through courier services. By contrast, most delivery services operate locally and some only in selected areas of their respective city. The high cost of physical retail infrastructure in urban centres is the main incentive for e-commerce and direct-to-home ventures. Other driving factors are the general spread of online media and e-commerce and a traditionally wide-spread popularity of home delivery. For consumers, delivery has the great advantage of saving time and logistical effort, especially where organic shops are not easily reached by consumers and product availability is unpredictable. Several informants in our study mentioned that they plan to start e-commerce in the future, which is another indicator of the great appeal and potential of this business model in the current market scenario in India.

4.7 General Trade and Organized Retail

The Indian retail sector underwent profound structural changes over the past few decades, which are often referred to as the Indian Retail Revolution. These structural changes happened in several phases[19]. In the first phase, small neighbourhood stores dominated the traditional urban retail market. The second phase began around the year 2000 with the opening of the first large malls, which usually include a supermarket or hypermarket. The current third phase of the retail revolution began in 2005/06. It is marked by a rapid increase in the number of supermarkets and an increase in the average size of stores, with a trend towards hypermarkets and larger malls. In 2007, organized retail only had a share of 4-5% of the total retail sector, and only 1% of food purchases took place in supermarkets. To date, the bulk of food purchases still takes place in kirana stores. At the same time, with 55% growth, organized food retail has the highest growth rate of all retail (IBEF 2008; Images Group 2009; Wiggerthale 2009). The share of organized retail is projected to increase to over 30% by 2013 (Assocham 2010).

---

19 For an overview of the history of retail in India since the 1980s, see Businessworld (2011).

Between 2006 and 2009, over 100 new supermarkets opened in Hyderabad (Srivastava 2009). Spar, the world's largest independent food retail chain, opened Hyderabad's biggest hypermarket to date of 20,000 square feet in Begumpet during that period[20]. New supermarkets, hypermarkets and malls are opening at an accelerating rate in the affluent neighbourhoods since 2008. This is a result of the increasing disposable incomes and lifestyle-orientation of young middle-class consumers, and their preference for shopping in a modern, secure, clean and air-conditioned environment. While shopping in traditional retail stores is a necessity of daily life, visits to malls and eating out in fast food outlets and up-market restaurants are increasingly perceived as a leisure activity. Supermarkets these days promise "to elevate shopping from a daily chore to a world class shopping experience that also offers value for money" (Reachout Hyderabad 2008).

To date, organized retail only holds a small market share of the total Indian retail sector. General trade – also referred to as unorganized or traditional retail – comprises kirana and general stores, convenience stores, street stalls, pavement vendors and pushcart vendors. It supplies the bulk of food purchased in urban centres, where only 1% of food purchases happen in supermarkets. Until recently, organic products were not available in traditional retail; in fact most kirana store owners are not aware of organic food. One exception is Mumbai, where a few long-standing kirana stores like Modern Stores in Pali Naka have been stocking products from the Mumbai-based organic company Conscious Foods since 1996. A small number of kirana stores in Mumbai included a limited number of organic products in their range in 2011. Organic companies such as Morarka Organic Foods and Conscious Food have actively expanded into the traditional retail segment in order to promote organic food consumption in the mass market. How many traditional retail stores will continue to stock organic in the longer run remains to be seen: Many shops listed on the Morarka Organic Foods retailer list in 2011 stopped selling organic products after a short while due to a lack of sales. The category of general trade also encompasses small-scale retail such as delicatessen specialty stores, sweets shops, bakeries and up-market restaurants or cafés that retail processed foods. The highest number of these stores is found in Mumbai, and their organic product range includes Indian organic brands as well as imported products.

---

20 At the end of 2012, all Spar outlets were taken over by the French chain Auchan, and the organic range was subsequently expanded to include more suppliers and a larger number of products.

Traditional retail stores in general trade are typically small and owner-managed, with a small number of employees. Their supply chains are a mix of local and India-wide suppliers, with products being sourced both from local small and medium enterprises and from distributors selling packaged products from India-wide corporate food processors. Gourmet specialty stores and delis by contrast mostly source organic products from premium domestic organic brands or imported organic products. These small retailers and kirana stores typically have a small organic range of less than 50 different products.

It has only been in the past three years that organic food became available in a growing number of modern format retail stores. However, availability has been growing rapidly and over time, organic products are likely to be available in most chains as well as independent supermarkets. The first organized retailers that started selling organic food products in India were privately-owned, large standalone supermarkets, for instance Q-Mart in Hyderabad, and regional or national chains. Spencer's was among the first supermarket chains that started stocking a sizeable range of organic products in 2007. Most India-wide supermarket and hypermarket chains now have an organic product range of varying size. Smaller local chains such as Balaji Grand Bazaar in Hyderabad only recently started selling organic products. While most retail chains stock organic products only in prime locations – based on customer profile and sales performance of organic products – others declared the goal of gradually making organic products available in all their outlets.

The range of organic products in modern retail stores varies greatly from one outlet to the next. Generally, supermarkets and hypermarkets have a much smaller range than organic specialty stores, typically less than 100 organic products and less than 2% of their total food sales. At present, their organic product range does not comprise organic fresh produce but only grains, pulses, spices, jaggery, dry fruits, honey and very few processed products such as breakfast cereals. Spencer's was the first supermarket chain that sold organic in-conversion vegetables in seven of their outlets in Bangalore as part of a cooperation initiative with ICCOA (see Case Study 7). So far, Spar and Nature's Basket are the only other supermarket chains that regularly sell organic fresh produce in selected outlets.

Organized retailers as a general rule stock only certified organic products that are properly labelled, and larger brands with professional branding and a wide product range. They operate with centralized India-wide supply chains, and while some of their suppliers are local small and medium enterprises, the bulk of packaged food products is either their own retailer brand or sourced from large corporate companies. Similarly, organic products are sourced from larger companies that have established efficient India-wide supply chains with local distributors or sales agents. Most organized retailers are not interested in procuring directly from small organic farmers, because it is difficult to ensure high product quality and consistent, timely and year-round supply. Supermarkets in India have not yet started to launch any organic retailer brands of their own.

Of the retail models we looked at, organized retail has the largest number of profit-seeking intermediaries involved in the supply chain. Therefore, the price levels either tend to be higher, and the share that farmers receive tends to be lower than in more direct distribution channels. Most organized retailers are incorporated as private limited companies. An exception is the cooperative supermarket chain Apna Bazaar in Mumbai which sells a small range of organic products in some of their outlets. While the retailer margin for organic product ranges from 15-25% among regular organized retailers, Apna Bazaar reported a margin of approximately 7%.

In our analysis of market shares in Bangalore (see Table 4-3), the total estimated share of organic food sales through organized retailers was 34.5%. This is slightly more than for organic specialty stores. However, if organic stores and non-food specialty stores such as Fabindia are taken together, they make up 56% of organic food sales – significantly more than organized retail.

5 Challenges and Success Stories in Organic Marketing

The demand for organic products is growing rapidly among urban consumers, and so are product availability and the number of stores in cities. In order to sustain and facilitate this growth, a number of challenges which stakeholders face in sourcing, distributing and retailing organic food have to be addressed. This chapter discusses the main obstacles that impede the development of the domestic market for organic food along the entire supply chain, from production and governance issues to consumer awareness and preferences. We present more examples and case studies of successful marketing initiatives, and summarize success factors and best practice examples for organic supply chains. In our research, we have found a great variety of approaches to solving the challenges involved in supplying to urban consumers.

5.1 Product Availability and Working with Suppliers

A major constraint in organic retail is the limited organic product range currently available in India. On the whole, most stores stock only dry provisions like grains, pulses, spices, jaggery, tea and coffee. Fresh fruits and vegetables as well as dairy products are not as readily available in urban markets, although availability has improved somewhat over the past few years. The biggest problems in organic fruit and vegetable supply chains in India are the limited number of organic producers, the lack of adequate storage and transport infrastructure, and the high risk for producers and retailers due to the perishable nature of produce. While non-perishables can usually be returned to the manufacturer in the event of spoilage or damaged packaging, retailers typically bear the entire cost of wastages of fresh produce. Most organic retailers do not have cold shelves, and in hot climates, some vegetables, especially green leafy vegetables, can wilt and rot in just a few hours. Several catering businesses use organic ingredients, but mostly not vegetables, because the supply situation is too unreliable. To date, no supplier of organic fresh produce can guarantee a reliable, consistent and high-quality year-round supply of fresh produce.

At the same time, the demand for fresh fruits and vegetables continues to be highest among all other organic food categories (Rao et al. 2006). Scientific studies, such as Ramanjaneyulu and Chennamaneni (2007) and Sinha et al. (2012), and media headlines have repeatedly pointed out the dangerous levels of chemical residues present in Indian vegetables. Accordingly, consumers' concern about food safety is particularly high for vegetables. This unmet demand constitutes a major opportunity for marketing safe organic produce, which a growing number of stakeholders are now beginning to take advantage of.

The availability of fresh produce varies considerably between the three cities we looked at, and within these cities. Organic vegetables are most readily available in Bangalore, which has favourable agro-climatic conditions and is an attractive market due to the relatively large number of organic stores and high demand from consumers. In Mumbai, organic vegetables started to become more readily available since 2010, with the start of the Farmers' Market and several delivery options. Since 2011, an increasing number of organic specialty stores also sell fresh vegetables.

Organic dairy products have more recently started to become available in some shops and through direct delivery, especially in Bangalore. Some of these dairy producers are certified, while others currently operate on a trust basis. Ghee has already been more readily available for some time, because it is not highly perishable and does not need refrigeration. A few producers have also started to market organic eggs in Bangalore. For instance, organic eggs and chicken meat are produced at the Lumiere farm and sold at their own restaurant and retail store in Bangalore.

The range of processed food products available in organic retail continues to be limited. Even in the non-organic sector, the bulk of food product sales in India are not processed (see Wiggerthale). In 2009, only 2% of all food products were processed, but the industry's target is to increase the share to 25% by 2025 (Wiggerthale 2009). The share of processed products is even less in the organic sector. Over the last few years, some established organic companies have expanded their range of processed products to some extent by developing products such as breakfast cereals, baby food, ready-to-eat snacks, jams and pickles. In addition, a few non-branded, uncertified processed products, such as peanut butter, pickles and preserves, puffed and flaked grains, sweets and snacks, are produced by various rural SHGs in cooperation with NGOs. These are produced with locally adapted small-scale technologies on the village level. The products are usually not certified organic, and it is sometimes unclear from the product labels whether all ingredients are organically grown.

Expanding the organic product range from currently approximately 1,000 products (Blume 2012) will be key to winning more consumers. A few organic companies claim to have a full typical Indian grocery basket of several hundred products available. On the retail shelf, however, this complete range is rarely ever encountered, and retailers complain that some organic manufacturers are able to supply only half of what they claim on their product lists.

Almost all respondents mentioned that ensuring a sufficient and regular supply of high quality products is one of the prime challenges in establishing organic food supply chains, especially for fresh produce. Most restaurants and caterers that use organic ingredients are unable to claim that they are 100% organic because organic vegetable supplies are not consistently available. Again, there are some regional differences: The organic caterer Organic Express found it much easier to source a regular supply of fresh organic produce in Gurgaon than in their Hyderabad branch. For commonly used ingredients such as tomatoes, good quality organic supplies are very difficult to source, which is why restaurants frequently resort to conventional produce. Restaurants with a fixed menu that is planned in advance do not have the security of supply in organic fresh produce that they would require. Therefore, they often sell meals as "made as far as possible with organically grown ingredients," a phrasing that gives them the freedom to use non-organic ingredients wherever organic is unavailable. They can also use uncertified products from producers whom they know personally to be growing organically without certification.

The limited organic supply has several causes. Firstly, only a limited number of farmers are able to supply organic products, and the majority of conventional farmers are not aware of organic agriculture. Secondly, while organic practices are often more labour-intensive, there is a general lack of farm labour in rural India. Thirdly, for fresh produce in particular, supply is limited because agro-climatic conditions do not permit to grow a wide range of crops in every region. Fourthly, a lot of organic produce does not reach urban markets due to logistical problems in the supply chain (see Chapter 5.3). And finally, farmers are not well trained in quality control, which makes it difficult to ensure consistent quality of produce, proper grading and reliable supply.

In order to improve their supply situation, organic processors and marketers have taken different measures towards backward supply chain integration. Commercially oriented organic companies have either built up their own production base on company-owned farms or tried to consolidate their relationships with a large number of farmers through contract farming arrangements or informal agreements. Most organic companies and retailers use a combination of various sourcing strategies. Most processing companies that have their own farms source additional raw materials from contract farmers, independent farmers or traders. Companies that use contract farming arrangements (cf. Chapter 5.2) often buy part of their products from independent farmers and traders. Cooperatives and producer companies source products from their member farmers; some of them exclusively, while others who have their own retail outlet also buy from other organic producers and companies. Corporate farming does not contribute much to domestic organic trade at present.

Organic companies and retailers try to expand their farmer base either by constantly scouting for new suppliers or by actively encouraging farmers to convert to organic production methods. The latter requires funding and the capacity to provide the necessary extension work, such as farmer trainings, monitoring of organic production standards and facilitation of internal control systems for organic certification. Farmers usually have better access to training and extension services if they have a long-standing relationship with an NGO or marketing organization. One organic company founder explained that farmers who are already certified usually have access to support and expertise, but that those out of reach of certification need more support and better access to extension services.

Much work goes into raising awareness and convincing farmers, because most conventional farmers are not aware of organic farming. Those who are new to it have to be convinced of its effectiveness, and they require training in organic farming methods and support in production and marketing. In many cases, extension services are provided through affiliated rural development NGOs that have worked in a particular area for a long time and have an established reputation in their region of operation. Some successful strategies for convincing farmers have been to demonstrate the feasibility of organic production on demonstration farms, and to let experienced organic farmers train other farmers. Many examples demonstrate that trust and long-term relationships between producers and organic marketing organizations – whether NGOs, organic processors or trading companies – are vital in establishing good and reliable working relationships with farmers. In community-supported agriculture initiatives, personal relationships between organizers, consumer members and producers are important for winning the farmers' trust and commitment.

Community-supported agriculture tries to solve supply constraints by consolidating a base of farmers who are closely associated with a group of consumers. Apart from ensuring regular supplies that match the demand, this strategy also helps farmers reduce risk and increase the marketability of what they grow. One of the basic ideas behind community-supported agriculture is that the risks of production and marketing should be borne by all stakeholders, including consumers – not just by the farmers or an NGO. Direct marketing and community-supported agriculture have started to successfully address the demand-supply gap for organic vegetables, albeit on a small scale. By avoiding intermediaries, these initiatives can substantially reduce costs and save farmers the troubles, risks and financial losses associated with middlemen. Farmers' markets and community-supported agriculture give farmers an assured market for their produce, and they often operate with fixed and cost-based prices, thus helping farmers avoid the risk of market price fluctuations.

In conventional vegetable supply chains, products are supplied by farmers in rural and peri-urban areas to local collectors and commission agents, from there to urban wholesale markets and finally to retailers and street vendors. If products are sourced from other parts of India, especially for supermarkets, the supply chain might involve even more intermediaries. In this system, a major share of the price margin goes to wholesalers and middlemen, and energy use for transport logistics and storage brings up the ecological footprint of food products. By avoiding intermediaries, the market value of organically grown produce from peri-urban areas is raised. In conventional supply chains, with several stages of intermediaries, these products lose much of their added value. Avoiding intermediaries thus increases the revenue for farmers and reduces consumer prices at the same time. According to several representatives of direct marketing initiatives and NGOs, around 30% of the end price in a conventional supply chain goes to the farmer, and their net profit after production costs is only 5-10%. By contrast, according to an expert interviewed for this study, the net profit for organic farmers selling through direct marketing can be as high as 80%.

The community-supported agriculture and direct marketing initiatives analyzed for this study give farmers an assured and viable marketing channel, providing an incentive to grow organic produce. This has in turn improved farm diversity and viability, and the long-term livelihood security of farmers. In the example of GORUS (see Case Study 4), all farmers develop detailed production plans together with GORUS staff before every planting season, based on an estimate of the demand for that season. MOFCA also employs a system in which production is pre-planned according to the number of subscribed consumers, and deliveries are prepaid for the entire season. This helps to minimize the risk of wastages, one of the biggest obstacles in organic fresh produce supply chains.

Among the non-tangible benefits of direct marketing is the enjoyment of personal interaction between farmers and consumers. The example of the Mumbai Farmers' Market (see Case Study 3) shows that meeting consumers who appreciate and value the additional efforts required in organic production and marketing can contribute immensely to the motivation of farmers to produce organically.

Another challenge that GORUS faced in expanding their farmer base is that many farmers are reluctant to make their farming system more complicated compared to mono-cropping of rice or sugarcane, since the vegetable plots need careful management and constant tending. On the farm level, GORUS is still working on developing standardization and efficient processes of production. For instance, farmers are expected to deliver on time and grade and sort produce at the farm; however, 80% of them regularly come late or with ungraded produce. The downside of the personal relationship to the coordinators and staff is that the discipline of farmers to comply with rules is sometimes low. GORUS is now thinking of introducing an incentive programme, a point system that rewards farmers who fulfil their supply requirements and entices them to work with more professionalism. Especially at the time of sowing and planting, the GORUS staff make frequent visits to the farms in order to ensure that the farmers grow what has been laid down in the planting plan.

5.2 Organizational Models and Legal Context

While commercial organic companies are usually incorporated as private or public limited companies, farmer-driven and non-profit marketing initiatives have to decide which organizational model and legal form of incorporation best suits their needs. Alternative options might be a producer company, a cooperative, a marketing wing of an NGO, or an informal association with a consumer club. Along the continuum from non-profit initiatives to commercial organic companies, there are several mixed forms. For instance, a few for-profit companies are associated with a non-profit organization, and many grassroots NGOs that facilitate the marketing activities of small farmers opt for a hybrid model of organization that combines a non-profit trust, foundation or society with a for-profit marketing organization. Such an arrangement allows the organization to access grant funding and tax exemption, which in turn enables them to provide agricultural extension services, technical assistance and capacity building to farmers as well as to support marketing activities through infrastructure and human resources. As such, the marketing activities are indirectly subsidized through the NGO. The Navdanya outlet in Mumbai, for example, is managed by volunteers, and several other NGO-supported marketing initiatives work with volunteers or staff paid by the NGO to support marketing activities.

For small marketing initiatives such as producer companies and community-supported agriculture groups, it is often difficult to access working capital. Funding is needed for many investments such as certification fees, storage facilities, processing technology, greenhouses, vehicles, plastic crates and other marketing infrastructure, and for brand development and promotion. Access to grant funding and affordable loans is especially important during conversion to organic and for start-ups in their first years, before the marketing of organic produce starts paying off and the company reaches the point of operational breakeven. Most small farmers do not have access to loans from banks, and the interest rates of commercial loans are too high for them. NSSO (2003) reports that 47% of small and marginal farmers get credit from informal moneylenders at prohibitive interest rates, and only 15% from banks.

In order to make capital available to farmers, GORUS has evolved a system in which consumers give small loans to farmers on a personal basis, and it has plans to develop a revolving fund for farmers. Additional funds are also needed for a seed bank and for farmer training. However, fundraising is a time-consuming effort, and most international funding mechanisms are accessible only to projects of a larger scale that impact hundreds of farmer families. In the case of Sahaja Aharam in Hyderabad, the producer cooperatives need more capital in order to expand the processed product range and scale up production volumes. So far, the cooperative has depended on commercial loans from the private capital market with very high interest rates. Investors in the agricultural sector are increasingly difficult to find, as are donors providing external funding. Therefore, the cooperative came up with the idea of setting up their own fund for farming investments. The financial viability of Sahaja Aharam's marketing model will be vital in supporting this effort in the future.

Unlike non-organic farming, there are no government subsidies available to organic farmers. Existing support programmes (see Chapter 3.3) reach only a small number of farmers, and most producers depend primarily on associated NGOs for access to capital, extension services and training. While support for organic farming in India was delivered mainly by the non-profit sector for a long time, the government has only begun to promote organic farming since the beginning of this century (Alvares 2009).

In Andhra Pradesh, a legislative provision for producer cooperatives under the Mutually Aided Cooperative Society (MACS) Act allows farmers to form a business enterprise for marketing that is owned and managed by the producers themselves. Similarly, producer companies are owned by farmers as the main stakeholders. The concept of producer companies was first introduced into the Indian Companies Act in 2003. The idea was to enable the incorporation of cooperatives as for-profit companies while also retaining the unique elements of the cooperative model within a regulatory framework similar to that of companies (Murray, no year). The concept did not become widely popular after its introduction, but has more recently seen a resurgence, with farmers starting to see the benefits (Bhosale 2011). Many farmer-owned companies see themselves as social enterprises, because their profit benefits resource-poor small and marginal farmers, and at least part of it is ploughed back into expanding the operations. Examples of organic producer-owned companies are Sahaja Samrudha in Bangalore, Chetna Organic in Hyderabad (see case study in Singh 2009: 138) and Timbaktu Organic in Anantapur District of Andhra Pradesh (see Case Study 5).

Case Study 5:

Farmer-Owned Success Story: Timbaktu Organic

The NGO Timbaktu Collective[21] operates in Anantapur District of Andhra Pradesh since 1991. It initiated an organic farming programme in 2005, with 300 farmer families on 1,650 acres of rainfed land. By 2012, the programme had grown to 1,050 families and over 5,000 acres. All these farmers are shareholding members of the Dharani Farming and Marketing Mutually Aided Cooperative Society Ltd. (Dharani FaM Coop Ltd.). This producer-owned company was registered in 2008 and is promoted by Timbaktu Collective. The farmer members together hold a share of 25% of the total capital of the company in the form of share capital and deposits. One of the main purposes of the producer company is to create value addition through processing and branding. The producer company owns a storage and processing facility, which procures the organic produce from the farmer members. Products are stored

---

21 Also see the case study in KICS and CWS (2012).

safely, processed and packaged under the brand name Timbaktu Organic. In addition to rice, millets and pulses, the product range includes millet flours, malts, and groundnut oil, butter and powder. These products are sold mainly in Bangalore as well as Hyderabad.

The organic farming programme was expanded from rainfed groundnut cultivation to other crops and to irrigated plots. It also promotes local cattle breeds and village-level seed banks. The producers have been using a PGS for organic certification, and in addition some members got externally certified by IMO. The success of the organic farming programme is also spreading into surrounding villages, where farmers are now taking interest, forming their own groups and attending the trainings offered by Timbaktu Collective. Dharani FaM Coop was able to break even with a small net profit by 2011. Together with a highly dedicated founding team, the support by external donors from within India and abroad was essential for the success of this initiative.

One of the challenges is the shortage of qualified staff for the producer company. As the Timbaktu Collective annual Report 2011-12 states, the farmer members' "understanding of business and larger market forces still remains insufficient" (Timbaktu Collective 2012: 14). Training programmes such as the Course in Rural Entrepreneurship and Management (CREAM), which was developed with the help of Timbaktu Collective, are therefore crucial for enhancing the capability of producers to manage their marketing enterprise and related activities successfully.

Based in Hyderabad, the Chetna Organic Agriculture Producer Company Ltd (COAPCL) started as an organic cotton grower initiative of farmers in Andhra Pradesh, Maharashtra and Orissa. Since organic cotton farmers produce various food crops like pulses and spices as intercrops, Chetna decided to also develop marketing channels for these products. The producer company is backed by the Chetna Organic Farmers Association (COFA), an NGO that supports the farmers. Chetna Organic manages the processing and packaging of produce, and it developed the brand "Zero" for NPM products.

Typical sales channels of farmer cooperatives, producer companies and NGO-driven marketing initiatives are bulk sales to organic processors and retailers as well as agricultural direct marketing (see Chapter 6.3). Some of them have also started opening their own small organic specialty stores (see Chapter 6.2). The examples of Timbaktu Organic and Chetna Organic demonstrate the vital importance of collectivisation as well as investing in product design, brand development and professional marketing for farmer groups. An important element in the success of these initiatives is the formation of farmer collectives for production and marketing (NAC Working Group 2013). Farmer producer organizations such as cooperatives and producer companies ensure ownership, autonomy and the participation of producers. They improve farmers' bargaining power in the market and allow them to retain more value addition by owning their storage and processing facilities and their own brand.

Support from an NGO is often crucial for the success of such farmer producer organizations, especially in the startup phase. This support can consist of financial and infrastructure input, guidance, staff time and the personal commitment by founding members. The NGO Navdanya, for instance, "has helped set up (...) the largest direct marketing, fair trade organic network in the country" (www.navdanya.org) which directly benefits small farmer groups. It also provides farmer trainings and promotes seed banks and biodiversity conservation. Other NGOs have also successfully facilitated direct marketing networks (see Chapter 4.4).

The Government of India circulated a Model Act on Agriculture Marketing to the State Governments in 2003. Until then, farmers were obliged to sell their produce through the official mandi system which is regulated by the State Agricultural Produce Market Committees (APMC). The aim of the amendment to the APMC Act was to help farmers achieve better prices by making alternative marketing channels available. In order to reduce their marketing risks and have greater price stability and financial security, farmers may choose to tie up directly with buyers through contract farming and buy-back arrangements with commercial buyers or to sell directly to consumers through farmers' markets and community-supported agriculture (see Chapter 4.4). The AMPC amendment makes contract farming legal and intends to protect the interests of farmers in contract arrangements.

Most of the projects detailed in Singh (2009) make use of contract farming arrangements. In our study, we found that only the larger companies in the domestic market work with contract farming and that all of them also employ several other sourcing strategies. In our sample, only 10 organic companies used contract arrangements in 2011, whereas 45 did not.

The APMC Act provides a model contract agreement, which is "quite fair in terms of sharing of costs and risks between the sponsor and the grower" (Singh 2009: 286). In reality, contract terms vary widely between different companies with regard to purchasing assurance, payment terms, provision of extension services and certification support. Not all companies give a guarantee that they will buy produce or provide support to farmers, and with few exceptions prices are tied to prevailing conventional market prices. These arrangements make farmers highly vulnerable to market price fluctuations. Contracts are usually made with individual growers and do not refer to group activities. Singh (2009) concludes that "the companies are interested in groups only to avail of lower cost certification in all cases and fair trade certification in some cases" (ibid: 292). Overall, contract arrangements tend to protect company interests at the cost of producers and do not cover production risks such as crop failure. NGOs also criticize the lack of community-involvement in contract farming.

Case Study 6:

Sahaja Aharam Organic Consumer and Producer Cooperative

The Hyderabad-based non-profit organization Centre for Sustainable Agriculture works with farmers' cooperatives across Andhra Pradesh to promote various aspects of sustainable rural development. In order to help farmers in marketing organically grown produce, Centre for Sustainable Agriculture developed the farmers' brand Sahaja Aharam, which in Telugu means "natural food". Centre for Sustainable Agriculture also serves as a facilitator between producers and consumers and helped to set up the Sahaja Aharam Mutually Aided Cooperative Federation, a federation of farmer cooperatives and an urban consumer cooperative.

Centre for Sustainable Agriculture initially concentrated on developing local markets in rural areas. In April 2009, the Sahaja Aharam Organic Consumer Cooperative was formed for marketing in Hyderabad, and the next year it opened a permanent organic food outlet on the ground floor of the Centre for Sustainable Agriculture office building. Initially, the NGO started its marketing activities in Hyderabad with a farmers' market on the office premises, but the cost of travelling to Hyderabad on a regular basis was too high for the farmers[22]. Instead, setting up a cooperative store that sources directly from producers turned out to be more economical. Since the launch of the cooperative store, the regular customer base has grown to over 150, and the range of products as well as availability of vegetables were also expanded gradually.

The bulk of produce is sourced from local farmers' cooperatives, located within a radius of 150 km around Hyderabad. All vegetables are seasonal; only wheat is sourced from Maharashtra, because it is not grown by the member

---

22 The government-introduced Rythu Bazaars are facing a similar problem; according to some speculations up to 75% of the vendors there are not actually farmers, as was originally intended.

farmers in Andhra Pradesh. Approximately 5,000 farmers are members of Sahaja Aharam. On average, each of them uses half an acre of their land to grow six or seven varieties of vegetables for the cooperative, in a mixed cropping model so that units can be rotated depending on market demand.

The cooperative has approximately 70 different products on sale, including 19 vegetable varieties. The store stocks almost all typical daily household needs, including some natural ayurvedic medicinal products. Approximately 50% of sales are vegetables, and the second most important product in terms of sales volumes is rice. The long-term goal is to expand the range of first- and second-level processed food such as flours. Apart from the store, the cooperative runs a vegetable delivery system which is more convenient for consumers and helps farmers in developing their production and business plans. Once a week, a cooperative-owned van runs deliveries to seventy households in a radius of 30 km.

The main target group for the consumer cooperative is the lower and upper middle classes. As Centre for Sustainable Agriculture notes, this differs from typical commercial organic shops, which are predominantly frequented by members of the upper middle and upper classes. Prices at the Sahaja Aharam outlet are lower than those in commercial organic shops and supermarkets; in fact, they are not more than 5-10% higher than non-organic products in the local market. These competitive prices are achieved by way of short supply chains without any intermediaries, by avoiding fees for third-party certification and by providing technical support for production and marketing to farmers through Centre for Sustainable Agriculture. In addition, the cooperative does not have to pay rent for retailing since the shop is in the Centre for Sustainable Agriculture office building. In the initial pilot phase of marketing, administrative work was backed by Centre for Sustainable Agriculture staff. Currently, four employees work full-time for the Sahaja Aharam marketing activities, and volunteers do about half of the work. In the long run, the goal is to use volunteers mostly for awareness raising activities and to run the core marketing activities professionally. In order to be viable, the mid- to long-term vision is to triple monthly sales and expand the member base from currently 300 to 3,000 households. Ideally, the purchase amount of each household would be INR 2,000 per month so that the system becomes financially viable. While only the most dedicated of customers come to the store in person, Sahaja Aharam is slowly spreading its presence across Hyderabad through delivery and since 2012 also through supplying to the Organic Bazaar and to specialty retailers.

There have been a number of challenges in developing the Sahaja Aharam marketing model, and Dr. Ramanjaneyulu, Director of Centre for Sustainable Agriculture, expects that the cooperative will take two or three more years to evolve a system that is fully functional and efficient. For one thing, the costs for transport, collection and distribution of vegetables are high: Delivery constitutes up to 15-20% of total costs because organic consumers are scattered across the city. At the same time, real estate has become very expensive, and most customers live in the more expensive parts of the city. Therefore, the cooperative decided to expand delivery and to start wholesales, rather than opening up more shops across the city. The cooperative is also thinking of changing the Sahaja Aharam brand name so that it can be used across different regions where this local name might not be understood.

Since the prospect of selling organic vegetables is highly promising, the cooperative wants to invest in a cold storage facility for the store in the future. This would help avoid losses, which now add up to 10% because of spoilage and pests. On the production side, the main targets for the near future are to work on a staggered model of planting, and to refine the system of multiple cropping. The cooperative is also planning to stock fruits and to expand the range of processed products. Processing will be done on a small scale to promote value-addition on the village level and help farmers move up in the value chain. One of the obstacles in processing is that it is difficult to get good technology for units of a smaller scale. This problem is similar to the challenge of marketing small farmers' produce: Since procuring larger volumes from few producers helps to cut costs, there are no established processes in India that support small farmers. Dr. Ramanjaneyulu concludes: "We need to re-invent all these things. See, buying from few and then selling to many, there's a model available. But buying from many and selling to many – that model is not worked out. That's what we are experimenting on."

5.3 Building Efficient Supply Chains and Retail Channels

Even in the non-organic food sector, the organization of the supply chain and the lack of adequate infrastructure for transport, storage and retailing are major constraints. In organic supply chains, these challenges are exacerbated by low volumes and irregular supply. Also, most organic enterprises in India are young and in a process of working out the best model for their supply chain by trial and error. The previous head of organic foods at Fabindia, Jashwat Purohit, says that the main issue in organic retailing is the supply chain: "This is a huge challenge; organic projects are scattered across the country and we are faced with many challenges – quality, consistency, transport, storage, shelf life – and so have had to partner with only very reliable suppliers who can consistently deliver the quality we want." (cited in Carroll 2005)

Logistical constraints, such as lack of roads, bad road conditions, lack of public transport options and high cost of transport, are part of the reason why organic fresh produce is not readily available in urban markets. The risks associated with sourcing highly perishable organic fruits and vegetables are very high due to damage and spoilage in the supply chain, from transport through storage and retailing. At present, transaction costs in organic supply chains are high because both producers and consumers are dispersed, production volumes are low and transport capacities are often not used efficiently.

Together with the lack of adequate transport infrastructure, long distances raise transport costs and make the timely delivery of perishable products challenging. For instance, the peri-urban fringe of a megacity like Hyderabad stretches up to 100-300 kilometres. In Mumbai – a metropolis of over 20 million inhabitants, spread across more than 60 km along the coast of Maharashtra – one of the biggest challenges of organizing the supply chain is the logistics of supply to and delivery within the city. It takes three to four hours to transport produce from peri-urban and rural areas into the city, after which it needs to be distributed in traffic which often comes to a gridlock during peak hours.

The Sahaja Aharam Organic Consumer Cooperative in Hyderabad found that it was not logistically feasible to deliver to each home individually because people are not always at home. As it would not be possible to deliver to more than 15-20 households in a day, all members are requested to pick up their produce at one of several collection points across the city. The cooperative is also considering the decentralization of distribution by outsourcing the actual delivery to local franchise stores across the city. These outlets could procure directly from the Sahaja Aharam farmers, use the brand name, store the produce and deliver it to individual homes. These franchise stores could be self-help groups, consumer cooperatives or individuals, and they would bear any marketing risks themselves. This option would only work once volumes have increased though. It would also require either tamper-proof packaging that guarantees organic product quality, or a high level of consumer trust based on personal relationships and a transparent supply chain.

Another major constraint in organic supply chains is the lack of storage infrastructure, especially cold storage. In hot climate conditions, vegetables can wilt within a few hours from harvest, often resulting in huge losses for farmers and retailers. There are no separate organic storage spaces offered on the commercial market, and organic companies and producer initiatives typically lack the funds to set up their own facilities. For many of them, this would not be feasible due to low volumes of organic produce. For non-perishable products like grains, pulses, potatoes and onions, several organic marketing organizations promote small-scale, traditional storage systems on the village level[23]. These low-tech, locally adapted systems require little capital and resource input, and they minimize the risks of wastages by protecting produce effectively from pests and spoilage. Such decentralized storage solutions promote food security and food sovereignty of producers. They also allow farmers to store produce until market prices are good, rather than having to sell immediately after the harvest.

In order to address the manifold logistical challenges, organic stakeholders have focused on organizing short supply chains for fresh produce that require minimum or no storage. While some invest in cold storage, most do not have the requisite financial resources and instead deliver produce to consumers within less than 36 hours from the time of harvest on the farm. The latter option is accomplished either through a system of selling vegetables in outlets only on particular days of the week, or through weekly home delivery. Short distances and fast supply chains with few or no intermediaries combined with backward supply chain integration and meticulous planning of production help to minimize wastages. Such systems require a reliable and committed consumer base, which can only be established and sustained if there is a consistent, high quality supply of a variety of vegetables. Community-supported agriculture initiatives achieve this by linking consumers directly with producers, ordering produce in advance and continuously improving their demand estimates.

The structure of agricultural markets is highly opaque, and small farmers lack market information as well as market access. Organic farmers are even known to have given up organic production methods again because it was not feasible due to lack of marketing opportunities. An example of successful buyer-seller facilitation for developing an organic vegetable supply chain is given in Case Study 7.

---

23 For some examples of storage techniques, see the annex in Ananthasayanan et al. (2013).

Case Study 7:

A Regional Label for Organically Grown Vegetables by ICCOA

The non-profit organization International Competence Centre for Organic Agriculture (ICCOA) works with farmers across India, supporting them in adoption of organic farming practices, in certification and market linkages. As part of these activities, ICCOA developed the label shown in Figure 5-1 for use on "Organically Grown Products" from Karnataka, mostly from horticulture projects that are in conversion for third-party certification. Their products cannot be officially marketed as "organic" before the conversion period is completed. It is essentially a label for regional produce, developed for the domestic market. The process of developing the label was based on insights gained through qualitative market research. During the process of developing the label, the core theme was food safety, but the label also communicates the key benefits of organically grown produce. The label also declares the source and regional origin. ICCOA lend their name as an assurance for "quality" and a mark of credibility to the claim of organic cultivation practices.

Organically Grown

Figure 5-1: Label developed by ICCOA for marketing organically grown vegetables from farmers in Karnataka

Source: ICCOA

ICCOA also facilitated the formation of the farmer society Organic Farmers Forum of Karnataka (OFFK), and assisted them in setting up a supply chain for marketing organically grown vegetables labelled with the ICCOA mark. Currently, these vegetables are sold in seven Spencer's supermarkets across Bangalore, and by two organic retailers, Dubden Green and Dharani. Plans are in the pipeline for starting a home delivery service for organically grown vegetables. However, since ICCOA is not a marketing agency, the idea is to get a private-sector entrepreneur involved in this activity. ICCOA's role would be limited to facilitating the supply from farmers. Another idea that is being discussed is to set up a pushcart model for selling organically grown vegetables in residential areas (cf. Chapter 5.4).

The vegetables are grown by farmers in peri-urban areas in Bangalore Rural District and surrounding districts. Grading is done directly on the village level by farmers or labourers. The quality expectations of retailers and consumers are high, and initially ICCOA had to give a lot of training on vegetable grading to farmers and labourers, but by now the grading works well. From the villages, produce is brought about 20 km to Bidlur village in Bangalore Rural District for packaging and labelling. Bidlur is centrally located between the two main peri-urban production centres and the Spencer's collection and distribution centre in Hoskote, 28 km from Bidlur. The vegetables are packed in the peri-urban production regions, and transported to the distribution centres of each retailer. Transportation is organised locally by ICCOA representatives, with the help of the buyers. All vegetables are either packed in plastic nets or labelled with a sticker. One of the reasons for packaging them is to prevent mix-ups with non-organic vegetables once the produce reaches the supermarkets.

One of the obstacles ICCOA faces in facilitating the supply of vegetables from farmer groups to supermarkets and organic stores is a mismatch of volumes and variety of vegetables that are supplied by the farmers on the one hand, and the requirements of retailers on the other hand. At this stage, farmers grow a limited variety of vegetables; all farmers in the ICCOA vegetable project together grow only around 12 different varieties, whereas modern retail chains demand a greater variety of around 24. Also, the volumes they require per vegetable are smaller than what the farmers would like to supply. The market for organic produce is limited, and retailers like to „play it safe" at this stage of development of the market, which means they would like to stock smaller volumes to reduce their risk. For the farmers, it would be easier and more profitable to grow and harvest larger volumes. An ICCOA staff member suggested that this might require a change in mentality on the part of the farmers, who would like to grow larger volumes of one variety rather than diversify their cropping system in order to meet the market demand.

Currently, the farmers working with ICCOA supply less than 100 kg per vegetable variety twice a week to retailers in Bangalore. For vegetables that are harvested regularly, farmers would prefer 200 kg every day; for those that are harvested in one go, like potato, larger quantities would be ideal. With the small quantities required at this stage, many farmers are reluctant to harvest, grade, pack and bring produce to the procurement centre. Another major challenge in the supply chain is the time and cost of transportation. Because of the small volumes, vehicle capacity is used only to 50-70%, bringing up the overall cost in relation to volumes.

ICCOA estimates that the vegetables reach approximately 1,000 consumers per month in Bangalore. In order to reach a greater number of customers, especially in supermarkets, more in-store promotion would be needed. However, the retail chains lack competent staff, and ICCOA does not have the capacity to dispatch staff for this task.

For the farmers, who get a 15% premium above the market price for their organically grown produce, it has been profitable to sell through this new marketing channel. They currently supply a total of 2 to 2.5 tonnes of vegetables every week. ICCOA is confident that the supply chain will become more efficient and financially self-supporting once the volumes increase further.

So far, the label developed by ICCOA is used only for produce from over 620 farmers, cultivating 900 hectares in surrounding areas of Bangalore. Their vision is for the label to be used for more farmers in the future, and to expand it into other regions of India. Potentially, it could grow into India's first label of a private-sector organic growers' association, providing an alternative to farmers who are in conversion for third-party certification.

In urban retail, a major economic constraint is availability and affordability of space. Real estate prices are highest in those areas where the majority of organic consumers and potential target groups are located: the prime locations of tier-I cities, such as South Mumbai and the Western Suburbs, Banjara Hills in Hyderabad, and Dollars Colony, Jayanagar and others in Bangalore. These constraints influence the choice of retail format and size of retail outlets. Independent organic specialty stores tend to be small and make efficient use of space, and some use their own premises, such as residential buildings and office buildings of NGOs. Others choose to forego physical retail space entirely by using retail formats such as e-commerce, mobile sales points and direct to home delivery, with storage space in less expensive parts of the cities. These increasingly popular solutions are also convenient for consumers in a setting where the density of organic retailers is low and traffic congestion deters many from travelling far. Also, home delivery of groceries and cooked food is generally quite popular in India.

E-commerce is a young phenomenon in India, not just in the food sector, and how well organic food consumers will take to it remains to be seen over the next few years. One potential obstacle in food e-commerce is that consumers like to see and feel products before buying them. Retailers who combine a physical retail outlet with an online purchasing portal find that many consumers first purchase in the shop and later on start ordering products online. The prospects of e-commerce are highly promising in a country with a consumer class that has speedily and enthusiastically adopted many new IT trends.

Conventional retailers such as supermarkets usually stock organic products in a category placement system, which means that all organic products are displayed on a shelf space that is labelled as the organic section. Organic specialty stores usually display their stock similarly, except that the bulk of a store's products are organic, and the non-organic products are placed in a separate section.

Over the past two to three years, most small organic retailers have started branding their own products, which they procure directly from farmers or in bulk from rural development organizations. This trend is partly a result of the lack of established organized supply chains, and partly due to the higher margins that can be achieved when purchasing in bulk. In some cases, the products are certified organic, but the organic label is not always displayed on the packaging. Packaging and branding is generally done manually in the store or warehouse.

Organic companies such as Morarka Organic Foods and Conscious Food have actively expanded into the traditional retail segment in order to promote organic food consumption in the mass market (see Chapter 4.7). How many traditional retail stores will continue to stock organic in the longer run remains to be seen: Many shops listed on the Morarka Organic Foods retailer list in 2011 discontinued organic products due to a lack of sales.

In conventional retail formats, be it general trade or organized retail, organic food reaches a very limited number of consumers. The organic category is usually not promoted, so that customers remain unaware of it unless they make an effort to find out more. Sales staff lack expertise regarding organic products and are unable to answer consumer queries (Radhika, Ammani, and Seema 2012). Organic stores tend to have a more personal approach to customer communication and can convey the quality differences of the organically grown produce more easily. However, since organic is still a small niche market, the customer base of these shops is limited compared to modern retail outlets.

A representative of Food Bazaar reported that using in-store promoters who could interact with customers right at the organic shelf boosted organic sales significantly. This clearly demonstrates that personal interaction is of crucial importance for increasing customer awareness, clearing their doubts about organic food and encouraging them to try it. It is not sufficient to stock organic products; a dedicated strategy and continued promotional efforts are required to bring up and maintain organic sales. It is important to raise awareness not just among consumers but also among conventional retailers and sales staff, and to train them so that they can guide customers competently.

In up-market specialty food stores and delis, consumers may be aware of organic food and willing to spend a premium. However, due to their exclusivity, these stores only reach a limited segment of consumers. By contrast, traditional retail channels like kirana stores, street stalls and mobile vendors reach a large number of consumers and therefore hold great untapped potential for organic sales.

5.4 Sustainability along the Supply Chain

One of the concerns in developing organic marketing models is how to manage supply chains sustainably, taking into account environmental, social and economic factors. A life-cycle perspective is useful in assessing the sustainability of different organic food supply chains, taking into account all major stages including production, transport, processing, packaging and retail. The concept of food miles, for instance, is a useful tool for comparing the performance of different supply chain models for the same product. It refers to the distance over which a product is being transported in the course of its production and distribution.

Organic supply chains are increasingly organized India-wide. Some of the larger organic companies have suppliers all over the country and even import some of their products. Most of the larger, India-wide operators process raw materials at a central location, and then ship the packaged products to distributors and retailers across several states. A few companies mentioned that they are making efforts to decentralize their supply chain models not only in order to reduce food miles but also to improve the economic efficiency of supply chains. Meanwhile, larger cities are seeing a growth of local food initiatives such as farmer cooperatives, agricultural direct marketing and community-supported agriculture, which aim to build local food networks and emphasize the values of eating locally, seasonally and organically. For these initiatives, food miles are again only one of several considerations; equally important are the transparency of shorter supply chains and a reconnection between the producers and consumers of food on a social level. Localized supply networks also tend to retain economic resources within the region of their production and to improve value addition by small local producers.

While geographical reach and food miles have a significant impact on the sustainability of a supply chain, transport efficiency can be equally important because it determines the food miles per unit of produce. In young and small-scale initiatives such as GORUS or MOFCA, transport costs are disproportionately high because delivery vehicles are often not loaded to full capacity (see Chapter 5.3). As volumes are scaled up to a certain extent, however, transport efficiency of the entire supply chain will improve.

Transport from retail outlets to the consumer's home also makes a significant contribution to overall food miles, especially because transport efficiency is extremely low at this stage. The decentralized location of organic outlets is therefore of prime importance, as are consumer habits such as the mode of transport chosen for shopping. If combined with eco-friendly modes of transport such as bicycles, cycle-rickshaws and pushcarts, direct-to-home could be a central component of climate-friendly local food supply systems. In fact, several stakeholders in the organic sector have expressed interest in cooperating for their vegetable deliveries with regular vegetable pushcart vendors, who already supply fruits and vegetables in many residential areas. To our knowledge, no one has implemented this model on a larger scale in the three cities of this survey.

Such pushcarts would have to be recognizably branded as organic, and a reliable system would have to be developed to ensure organic product quality and rule out mix-ups. Building accountability would require long-term relationships between vendors and organic producers, training for vendors to develop an understanding of organic principles, and active participation to give vendors ownership of the business model. The pushcart concept has great potential in a context where a large number of consumers already purchase vegetables regularly from pushcart vendors and road-side stalls. Decentralized and mobile marketing of organic fruits and vegetables could reach consumers who are not willing to make an effort to go to an organic store regularly or to order organic home delivery.

In addition to transport, a major part of the energy consumed in the life-cycle of a food product is used for processing. The higher the level of processing, the more energy-intensive the product becomes. The organic food range available in India to date is mostly comprised of products that are minimally processed, such as milled grains and pulses, ground spices and oil. A smaller range of processed products such as flours, puffed grains, jams, pickles, spice mixes and spice pastes are available from organic companies and from rural self-help groups or farmer groups. Very few highly processed products, such as breakfast cereals, snacks, biscuits, and ready-to-eat items, are available from a small number of brands. Some organizations like Timbaktu Organic (see Case Study 5) have made technologies such as oil mills available to producer groups, thus retaining more value addition on the village level rather than passing it on to processing companies that buy in bulk and produce for either the domestic or export market. Similarly, GORUS farmers use adapted small-scale technology like a solar drier and manual pulping machine to process any produce that is left over. By promoting value addition on the farm level, farmers can reap a greater share of the organic premium compared to selling unprocessed raw materials.

The more a product is processed, the more elaborate the packaging usually becomes, thus contributing to urban waste problems in addition to consuming more energy. Plastic is the preferred packaging solution of almost all retailers, whether organic or non-organic, because of low cost, light weight and ease of handling. Open sales of products like grains, pulses and spices are rarely encountered in the organic sector anymore. One organic store in Bangalore that sells products openly found that, in the end, products were still sold in plastic because consumers did not bring their own containers. A few stakeholders have experimented with paper and glass as well as reusable bags and containers. While there are several problems – glass has a high weight and breaks easily; paper bags reduce shelf life, might tear in transport and do not protect from humidity; laminated paper is costly – a number of organizations have demonstrate that non-plastic solutions can be worked out if sufficient care is taken in transport, storage and handling.

Some stores claim that they use biodegradable plastic for packaging and carry bags. Upon inspection, we found that these claims are not always truthful. In at least one case, the material used was in fact oxo-fragmentable plastic, which is even more harmful in the environment and in recycling processes than conventional plastics (European Bioplastics e.V. 2009).

Several organic retailers reported that their customers frequently request plastic-free packaging solutions. At the same time, consumers show little willingness to make an effort to support such efforts. Stakeholders that made an effort to reduce packaging in their home delivery systems, for instance through reusable boxes, crates and bags, encounter non-cooperation of customers who do not return the containers. The Sahaja Aharam Organic Consumer Cooperative, for example, initially delivered in reusable crates but found many consumers unwilling to return the crates. Any delivery system trying to operate in an eco-friendly manner will face this problem, at least until a mindset of routinely returning containers – as used to be the case with the old milk bottle system – is re-established in consumers' mindset. Even for buying vegetables in organic stores, some customers do not bring their own bags and expect to be given a cloth carry bag. GORUS delivers in plastic crates that are immediately emptied and taken back. While this system does take precious extra time during delivery, it also ensures that the crates are returned duly. GORUS also packages pickles and jams in reusable bottles, but hardly any of the customers actually return them, in spite of a deposit fee. Using paper bags for delivery was found not to be feasible because they become wet and break, and biodegradable plastic solutions are too expensive.

5.5 Certification: Opportunity or Obstacle?

Third-party certification provides an important mechanism of quality assurance in a context where consumers are far removed from the sites of agricultural production, both in export and the domestic market. In India, the organic standards and India Organic label were developed specifically for the export of organic products[24]. Certification and labelling are not yet mandatory for selling organic products in the domestic market (cf. Chapter 3.3). Many farmers and NGOs do not aim for third-party certification and the India Organic label because the certification fees are considered unaffordable for small farmers. While per-hectare financial support for conversion to organic is available in several state and central government schemes (Menon, Sema, and Partap 2010), most small farmers do not have access to certification support from any government programmes, organic companies or NGOs. Also, the paperwork and formal structures required for documentation are time-consuming and an obstacle especially for illiterate farmers. While the organic label would give small farmers equal access to organic markets and premiums, the fees and documentation requirements for third-party certification are the main obstacles preventing them from applying for certification (Garibay and Jyoti 2003).

---

24 See Chapter 3.3 for an outline of the Indian organic standard and certification schemes for third-party certification and Participatory Guarantee Systems.

A few organic companies and NGOs fund certification costs for farmers and facilitate the process of setting up farmer groups for internal control systems (ICS). However, the majority of farmers do not have access to external support for certification, which is a particular challenge in the conversion period when yields may be lower and no organic premium can be charged yet. As an alternative to third-party certification for small farmers, many rural development NGOs and farmer cooperatives work with Participatory Guarantee Systems (PGS). PGS systems are based on participatory principles, have a higher degree of community ownership and farmers have to pay only a small fee in order to get certified (Misra 2009, cf. Chapter 3.3).

Another quality assurance mechanism used by producer groups and companies is the commissioning of independent laboratory sample tests to guarantee that vegetables do not contain any pesticide residues. Some brands explicitly reject certification but have nonetheless gained the trust and loyalty of aware consumers because they operate on the basis of long-term personal relationships and transparent supply chains. One example is Navdanya, which, instead of certification, gives the "Navdanya Guarantee" on products that are sourced from small and marginal farmers in the NGO's network. The retail chain Fabindia uses a company-owned three-tier labelling system for products that are certified organic, in conversion and natural, because not all products are available from certified suppliers (see Case Study 2). ICCOA also developed a private-sector label that is used on organically grown, in-conversion vegetables grown by farmer groups in Karnataka (see Case Study 7). Chetna Organic developed the non-pesticide management (NPM) initiative Safe Harvest Pvt. Ltd. and the brand "Zero", which guarantees zero pesticide use through a PGS group certification process. Eighty percent of the produce is organic and the rest NPM in conversion to organic. Nevertheless, in the Indian market, Chetna sells all products as NPM rather than certified organic, to avoid complications, to better suit the requirements of small producers and to reach a greater number of consumers.

At the same time, organic companies increasingly use third-party certification in order to assure consumers who are far removed from the sites of agricultural production that products are genuinely organic. Dholakia and Shukul (2012) found that one of the barriers to organic buying is that consumers are unable to recognize products as organic due to lack of labelling. Many consumers found it "difficult to judge a true organic product" (ibid: 225, cf. Rao et al. 2006). The majority of consumers in India – even those who buy organic products – are not aware of certification and do not recognize organic labels. The organic standards, certification system and India Organic label were developed mainly with export markets in mind, and there has never been a coordinated consumer education campaign for either the India Organic label or PGS.

In the study conducted by Roy et al. (2010) with consumers in Mumbai, about half of the respondents said they looked for certification on food that is sold as organic. Osswald and Dittrich (2010) found in their survey in Hyderabad that only 10% of all respondents had seen the India Organic label before, and 8% the PGS Organic India Council label. Familiarity with labels was only up to 12% higher among those respondents who regularly or occasionally purchased organic. The authors also found that even among those who had seen the label before, the vast majority were not sure of its meaning. As with general awareness of organic farming, knowledge about certification and labels is highest among higher-income and more educated groups. The majority of Indian consumers are not familiar with the meaning of various food labels such as ISI mark, Agmark or FPO (Fruit Products Order) license (Polasa et al. 2006; Sudershan et al. 2008a; Sudershan et al. 2008b).

Another challenge in organic retailing is the fact that not all consumers trust third-party certification agencies or anonymously awarded labels. Three-fourths of the consumers interviewed by Osswald and Dittrich (2010) expressed a general confidence in organic labels. At the same time, personal relationships and trust in producers and brands generally play a much more important role in Indian food retail than labels do. The distrust in certification has to do with several factors, including unfamiliarity with the concept, suspicions of corruption in an anonymous marketing context, weak consumer laws and a lack of legal remedy in case of violations. Accordingly, in addition to PGS, a significant number of non-certified products are sourced directly from farmers by NGOs and retailers on the basis of personal relationships, trust and transparent supply chains. Stakeholders in the grassroots organic movement, such as producer companies, direct marketing and community-supported agriculture, rely on PGS and on personal interactions between farmers and consumers to build trust in organic. Many expressed more faith in "knowing their farmer" than in the anonymous and distant mechanism of third-party certification. Direct marketing initiatives give producers and consumers an opportunity to interact with each other directly, thereby enhancing mutual trust and confidence in organic production standards while avoiding the cost of third-party certification. Through local food networks and community-supported agriculture in particular, consumers have the opportunity to reconnect with the sources of food products and the people who grow them. They can also learn more about organic production methods during farm visits (Kneafsey et al. 2008).

Many organic consumers clearly associate larger brands, such as Fabindia, 24 Mantra (Sresta Bioproducts) or Down to Earth (Morarka Organic Foods), with organic food. Consumer trust in these brands is generally high. Not all regular buyers of these organic brands are necessarily aware that the products they are buying are certified or that a system of organic certification exists in India at all. On the other hand, many consumers assume that certain brands, companies, NGOs or shops are fully organic, even though none or not all of their products actually are. One of the reasons for this confusion is the low level of awareness of organic certification and labels, which means that many consumers are not sure how to verify if a product really is organic. They also have little knowledge about organic production standards, and information given by sales staff is often incorrect and misleading. Consumers may have greater trust in particular brands, organizations and personal contacts as opposed to an anonymous third-party certification process.

The other reason for the confusion about whether shops and products are genuinely organic lies in misleading terminology. Many organic companies and shops promote their non-organic product range as "natural," a term that lacks any established definition or protection. While some use the word "natural" to refer to products from natural farming[25], others simply refer to products with certain health claims, such as being free from artificial preservatives, colouring agents and flavours, although the ingredients may have been produced in a conventional, chemical-based farming system. In some contexts, the term "natural" refers only to the level of processing, meaning that a product does not contain ingredients like refined sugar or flour. "Natural" in this context is easily confused by consumers and even sales staff with other terms such as "pure," "fresh," "farm-fresh," "healthy" and "free from additives". These terms are also used in the names and promotional materials of both organic and non-organic companies and shops. Many consumers are not aware that the "natural" tag does not usually imply that a product is grown in a natural farming system, and hence take it to mean organic or of an equal standard. This confusion is particularly dangerous in a context where consumers have little knowledge about either nutrition or organic farming. Some of the reasons why organic stores stock such "natural" products are the lack of a large product range in

---

25 See definitions in Chapter 3.1.

organic quality at present, inconsistent supply and the low quality of organic produce.

Apart from organic certification, only a few organic brands in India are Fairtrade certified, and they mostly produce organic cotton, textiles or other export crops, such as spices, coffee and tea. For instance, Chetna Organic (Hyderabad), Zameen Organic (Hyderabad) and Vasundhara Agri Horti Producer Company Ltd. (VAPCOL, Pune) are certified by Shop for Change. Indian consumers are even less aware of the Fairtrade concept and associated labels of than the organic label. Very few fair-trade organic food products that are grown and processed in India are available in the domestic market, with a few exceptions like honey or coffee. Ironically, the only branded Fairtrade certified organic food products that are available in the domestic market are imported ones, for instance brown sugar imported from the UK for sale in upmarket supermarkets where the product range is dominated by imported products. Godrej Nature's Basket and Foodworld Gourmet in Bangalore are examples of such stores.

The Fairtrade standards implemented in export production benefit the farmers overall, even though the products they grow for subsistence and for the domestic market may not be Fairtrade certified. There are several Fairtrade certified organic cotton and garment producers that sell in the domestic market. A few of them also market organic or NPM food products, although these are not Fairtrade certified and labelled. While very few domestic organic producers are Fairtrade certified, many organizations claim to apply similar principles to their relationships with farmers and their marketing activities, for instance paying above average prices and passing on a higher share of the organic premium to farmers.

5.6 Building Awareness and Meeting Consumer Needs

A number of surveys were conducted among consumers in various parts of India to find out about awareness levels, motivations and hindrances for organic food purchasing. Two of the major challenges in reaching more organic consumers are the lack of awareness and the difficulty of meeting consumer needs regarding product range, availability, quality and price. Although awareness of organic is spreading in India and the topic has begun to receive more attention from the mainstream media, there is still a huge unmet need for information among consumers. Garibay and Jyoti (2003) found that lack of awareness is the main reason why more people do not buy organic products in

Mumbai. The majority of the population is not aware of the harmful effects of non-organic agriculture and of the existence of organic farming. Among those who are aware of and interested in organic, there is a lack of information on where organic products can be purchased. To date, there is no comprehensive, up-to-date and user-friendly online directory of organic food retailing in India.

According to a survey conducted by Garibay and Jyoti (2003), 25% of consumers in Mumbai had heard of organic food. A Technopark Report on Food Habits of India from 2009 found that 41% of consumers are aware of organic food (cited in Datta 2010). Another study by Menon, Sema, and Partap (2010) compiled figures from AC Nielsen Org-Marg and Rao et al. (2006) and calculated that while 18% of consumers are aware of organic food, only 10% actually consume it. Dholakia and Shukul (2012), on the other hand, found in a 2008 consumer survey of 110 homemakers in Vadodara in Gujarat that over 80% of their respondents had "good knowledge about organic food" (ibid: 221).

These vastly different percentages are a result of different study designs, and the different socio-economic profiles of the populations included in the surveys. Thus, the higher estimates are not representative of the overall population. Osswald and Dittrich (2010) found in a survey of consumers in different parts of Hyderabad that 75% of respondents on average had heard of organic food and had a basic understanding of its meaning. A comparison between different localities and socio-economic groups revealed that awareness was highest among groups with a higher socio-economic background and education level, especially those who have lived abroad and got to try organic food there as well as expatriates. Among the vast majority of the population, awareness levels are much lower. A survey of supermarket customers in Hyderabad conducted by Lohr and Dittrich (2007) showed that 76% had never heard of organic food, and only 3% had ever purchased it. Those that were aware of organic food all had an upper middle class background.

A number of studies have concluded that for those consumers who are aware of organic food, limited product availability is one of the major purchasing barriers (Rao et al. 2006; Chakrabarti and Baisya 2007; The Nielsen Company 2007; Chakrabarti 2010). Organic products are available in a limited number of stores, and these are often concentrated only in selected parts of a city. Most supermarkets and kirana stores do not yet sell organic products, although availability in supermarkets is rapidly improving. Retailers are currently not able to offer a complete range of food products. Fresh fruits and vegetables have the most limited availability, and retailers usually only sell them on one or two days of the week. Consumers who have purchased organic food abroad are familiar with the wide range available in supermarkets in developed organic markets, and expect a similar range in the Indian market. Organic companies and retailers are making efforts to expand their product range but are struggling with a lack of supply, especially for fresh produce. Some consumers are reluctant to buy only partly organic and would prefer to "switch" their entire food sourcing to organic. Hence they want to be sure that the same products will be consistently available in the long run. GORUS in Pune (see Case Study 4) realized that their model of vegetable box deliveries is only attractive if consumers can get at least 80% of their weekly vegetable requirements from the GORUS basket. Consumers mostly expect a variety of 25 to 30 different vegetables.

In addition to supplying a wide product range, organic retailers are also struggling to guarantee a consistent product availability and quality, especially for fresh produce. These challenges are due to difficulties in coordinating with producers and seasonal fluctuations of product availability (cf. Chapter 5.1), as well as logistical challenges such as inadequate transport infrastructure and storage space (cf. Chapter 5.3). In community-supported agriculture and delivery schemes that supply a basket of seasonal vegetables, some consumers have complained that the variety of vegetables is too small, whereas the quantity of particular vegetables is too large while they are in season.

Organic stakeholders use several strategies to improve product availability. As part of a strategy of backward supply chain integration, stakeholders tie up with organic producers, provide training for farmers and assist them in demand-based production planning. These activities can improve the product range, make the supply flow more reliable and ensure better quality control by farmers. The community-supported agriculture initiatives we interviewed are in a process of learning which vegetables will be most in demand so that they can help farmers to make better planting plans.

Organic companies and retailers with India-wide or international supply chains are trying to expand their product range so that it will eventually equal what consumers are used to from conventional retail. While grassroots initiatives and small retailers also try to expand the product offering – for instance by cooperating with producers in other regions, expanding their storage capacity or investing in greenhouses to extend the growing season – they also promote local and seasonal eating habits. Farmers are encouraged to grow crops and varieties that are well-adapted to local agro-climatic conditions. Local and seasonal produce are proactively marketed to consumers as part of a sustainable and enjoyable food lifestyle.

Consumers in urban India have gotten used to a year-round supply of a wide variety of food products at street stalls and in supermarkets that are sourced locally, nationally and internationally. Awareness of the seasonality of agricultural produce is declining, especially in the younger generation. One of the objectives of community-supported agriculture is to re-educate consumers about eating locally and seasonally: "We are spoilt for choice. We think only mangoes are seasonal. So, yes, the participating consumers will have to relearn a lot in terms of their eating habits," says Neesha Noronha, one of the organizers of MOFCA's Hari Bhari Tokri (quoted in Ansari 2010). By supplying a mixed basket of seasonal vegetables, box delivery schemes give urban dwellers an opportunity to reconnect with natural cycles of agricultural production and to obtain fresh, nutritious vegetables.

While some vegetable delivery schemes give customers a chance to order individual products and quantities from a list every week, others supply a pre-determined mixed basket of seasonally available vegetables. The former system requires good production planning, weekly adaptations of the produce list and online order form, and significantly more labour for packing the personalized crates. Nevertheless, GORUS's experience in Pune showed that many consumers prefer being able to choose rather than receive a fixed basket. Kneafsey et al. (2008) explore the interesting notion that consumers may in fact find the pre-determined mixed basket option more convenient, because it saves them from having to make shopping choices while at the same time guaranteeing a great variety of produce. The authors point out the difference between choice and variety – while customers at a supermarket have a lot of choice from an overwhelming product range, the obligation to choose often means that consumers end up buying the same products year round. By way of getting a mixed basket delivered, people end up eating a greater variety of food, and they tend to try more new products and varieties than they normally would.

Apart from product availability, price has been mentioned as a major constraint preventing consumers from buying (more) organic food. While there are significant price differences within the organic sector, organic food is still priced significantly higher than conventional food. Garibay and Jyoti (2003: 17) found that organic products in department stores in Mumbai cost up to twice as much as non-organic ones, and another study found that "organic food is priced over 25% more than conventional food in India" (Organicfacts 2006).

According to Rao et al. (2006), the organic premium in urban markets is 15-30%. It should be pointed out here that a comparison of organic and conventional price levels is only convincing if organic products are compared with non-organic products of similar quality, rather than with the cheapest available products.

Prices for organic products vary significantly between different companies, different retail formats and across product categories (Osswald & Dittrich 2010). Generally, prices are lower when fewer profit-seeking intermediaries are involved in the supply chain. Overall, farmers only benefit from premium prices where an NGO is involved in marketing (Partap and Vaidya 2009). Unbranded and uncertified organic products from local producers, marketed directly from farmers, through NGOs or small organic stores, are often priced much lower than the average of branded organic products. Price levels of the larger organic brands vary widely, and overall tend to be higher. The Hyderabad Agricultural Cooperative Association (HACA) has an agreement with the farmers selling NPM vegetables in their outlet that the prices may not be more than 2-3 Rupees more per kg than the prices fixed by the government for conventional produce. However, the farmers claim that they would need an additional 2-3 Rupees in order to fully cover their production costs.

Several organic companies and marketing initiatives actively try to make organic food available at affordable prices, so that it can reach a broad spectrum of consumers. Furthermore, some grassroots organizations have a fair pricing policy that guarantees higher prices for farmers and encourage consumers to pay a slightly higher price in turn. Part of their mission is to educate consumers about the importance of paying a fair price so that farmers can build secure and sustainable livelihoods. The price levels in community-supported agriculture can also be significantly lower than for certified organic products in specialty stores because they operate with short supply chains, direct marketing and participatory guarantee systems instead of third-party certification. In those cases, the price differential becomes a question of good communication: If consumers are convinced that the premium they pay translates into a fair price for farmers and high quality products, many will be ready to pay more.

Thakur and Sharma (2005, cited in Singh 2009) found that awareness, preference and demand for organic food are on the rise. Thus, as organic trade volumes go up, industry experts expect that prices will come down further. During the launch of the Organic Trade Association of India, Mukesh Gupta (OTA President, quoted in Oneindia 2010) stated: "Organic produce is no more considered an elitist product." He also added that, for most food products, wholesale prices are already only 10% above the conventional level, and retail prices 15-20%. A representative of Sresta Bioproducts said in 2010 that products were "priced 30-40% higher than conventional products, and expected to come down to 10-15% in the long run" (Osswald and Dittrich 2010).

Table 5-1: Empirical studies on consumer perceptions and willingness to pay

Authors	Location	Findings
Dholakia and Shukul (2012)	Vadodara (Gujarat)	71% of respondents mentioned high cost as a hindrance
Kriesemer, Weinberger, and Chadha (2009)	Kolkata (West Bengal), Ranchi (Jharkhand)	41% of respondents were willing to pay more for safely produced vegetables, especially for certified organic vegetables
D. Roy et al. (2010)	Mumbai (Maharashtra)	Respondents rated nutrition, safety and taste as significantly more important characteristics of food products than price
Radhika, Ammani, and Seema (2012)	Hyderabad (Andhra Pradesh)	14% of respondents were not ready to pay a premium, but 61% of replies were neutral, and only 25% were ready to buy organic products at a high price
Osswald and Dittrich (2010)	Hyderabad (Andhra Pradesh)	Only 25% of those consumers who do not buy organic think that the prices are too high
Morarka Organic Foods consumer survey, cited by Heinze (2012)	10 cities across India	> 30% of respondents would like to buy organic products and are prepared to spend 10-20% more for them

Table 5-1 gives on overview of several empirical studies on consumer perceptions conducted in different cities across India. Overall, they conclude that higher prices are not a major constraint for health-conscious consumers, provided that the product quality is adequate (Dholakia and Shukul 2012; Radhika, Ammani, and Seema 2012; D. Roy et al. 2010; Osswald and Dittrich 2010). Most respondents in the survey by Radhika, Ammani, and Seema

(2012) were satisfied with the taste and product quality of organic food. In the same vein, a newspaper report on organic vegetable sales in 2009 stated that "customers do not mind paying for healthy vegetables" (The Hindu 2009). The majority of consumers have other reasons for not buying organic, for instance because they are not readily available, appearance is found to be less attractive than non-organic products, and products are often not properly labelled and thus not recognizable as organic. Many consumers expressed doubts about product authenticity, and the majority of consumers are not aware of organic certification and labelling (see Chapter 5.5).

Even consumers in the higher socio-economic segments are price sensitive with regard to food, and the majority of consumers – both buyers and non-buyers of organic food – perceive organic as being more expensive than non-organic. Although awareness of and demand for organic food are growing among consumers, Dr. Ramanjaneyulu of Centre for Sustainable Agriculture reckons that even a 5-10% higher price would make a big difference and potentially deter customers. At the same time, in light of the increase in average disposable incomes of the urban population, spending more on organic food often amounts more to a matter of priorities than of actual purchasing power. An Ernst & Young (2006) report stated that between 1995 and 2005, the number of urban upper and middle class households increased by 16%, and their discretionary spending rose by 20%. As part of this development, consumer preferences are also changing, with more and more consumers preferring higher quality goods, and a greater willingness to pay higher prices for these. At the same time, the share of food in average total household spending is continuously declining in India – from 56% in 1995 to an estimated 34% in 2015, and 25% in 2025. By contrast, health care expenditure is projected to increase from 4% in 1995 to 13% in 2025 (Ablett et al. 2007). Part of this increase will be due to diseases that are related to food and lifestyle.

Organic consumers have a monthly income that is significantly above average (D. Roy et al. 2010). Radhika, Ammani, and Seema (2012: 67) found that organic food consumers in Hyderabad "mostly belonged to wealthy classes, were highly health conscious, and a mix of professionals and businessmen." The typical organic consumer is urban, educated, and from a middle or high-income household. These consumers, who are mostly in the SEC A and B segment with average household incomes of over INR 10,000 per month (Datta 2010), can afford to demand quality in food. In lower income groups, however, price does remain a strong concern. Osswald and Dittrich (2010) conclude: "Although a small number of highly dedicated consumers are willing to make considerable efforts in order to purchase organic products, the majority of consumers are not prepared to compromise too much on convenience or price levels." (ibid: 57)

Finally, another constraint that emerged from our research is a lack of professionalism in marketing and customer communication often displayed by organic companies and retailers. A lot of organic stores covered in our outlet survey provided a very pleasant shopping experience, with carefully designed shop interiors using natural materials such as wood, and a good product range including fresh vegetables. However, others had problems such as dusty shelves, disorderly product display and empty shelves due to lack of product availability. Among the many examples of a lack of professionalism in customer communication are spelling mistakes in leaflets, inaccurate claims about organic farming and product properties, misleading addresses on websites, dysfunctional websites, wrong phone numbers and unreliable and inconvenient opening times. Sales staff frequently show a lack of competence and commitment. For instance, their knowledge about organic farming, certification and product properties is often inadequate; billing is often slow and fraught with problems such as lack of change; and for products that are not labelled, many shop attendants in our survey were even found to be unable to answer whether the product is organic or not. Organic stores sometimes make misleading and inaccurate claims about product properties, and products sold as "natural" may be mistaken for organic products, especially when they are not certified and consumers are unaware of certification (cf. Chapter 5.5). Wherever the store owners are present in the store, consumers can get much better background information about the products and organic farming in general. A few organic companies have started to systematically collect feedback on overall customer satisfaction and new products in order to improve their offering.

Case Study 8:

"Greens in a Box": MOFCA's Hari Bhari Tokri

In 2009, fresh and locally grown organic vegetables were difficult to come by in Mumbai. In response, a group of organic farmers located in peri-urban areas of Mumbai got together with activists of Mumbai's organic movement and a number of conscious consumers who were keen on a regular supply of organic vegetables. They started the Mumbai Organic Farmers and Consumers Association (MOFCA), an organization that now organizes weekly deliveries of a mixed basket of vegetables known as Hari Bhari Tokri – or "Green Full

Basket". The initiative aims to be more than a supplier of fresh, local, seasonal and organically grown produce. As one of the organizers puts it: "We are not just another vegetable vendor." One of the primary aims of MOFCA is "to place people before profit in the production of food." Toward this goal, they have established direct relationships between the people who grow food and those who eat it, thereby supporting local farmers as well as supplying good and affordable food to urban consumers. The three primary goals of the tokri scheme are to demonstrate and share sustainable farming techniques, to create an alternative market model with shared risks and fair prices for farmers and consumers, and to educate consumers in order to create and sustain demand for seasonal, local and organic food. By becoming shareholders in the cooperative, consumers and producers share the risks involved in any agricultural production system.

In the first season, vegetables were sourced from seven farmers. By 2012/13, the number grew to 35 small and marginal farmers and 4 urban farmers who cultivate a total of 8 acres of vegetables for the tokris. The farms are located near Mumbai, the furthest one at a distance of approximately 200 km. Until now, the organizers selected the participating farmers on the basis of personal trust. As the system gets scaled up, they envision employing a Participatory Guarantee System (PGS) that would involve producers and consumers in monitoring organic production methods. In an interview, Ubai Husein, one of the founders of MOFCA and a supplying farmer, explained that "a check is important because the integrity of the group rests on the integrity of each farmer". The main purpose of the PGS would be to monitor production processes and establish documentation practices with the farmers, and not so much for getting an organic label.

Integrity and transparency are core values of MOFCA: The partnership terms for participating in the scheme are accessible on the internet, and consumers have the opportunity to visit the farms at any time in order to see the production methods for themselves. So far, few consumers have made use of this opportunity, and Ubai Husein speculates that customers either do not have the time in their busy Mumbai lives, or they already know the farmers and the organizers personally and trust them without having seen the farms. In monsoon season 2012, 250 consumers held a farm share and received tokri deliveries. Even though MOFCA only promotes its activities through word-of-mouth and informal email lists, another 800 consumers are already on a waiting list, which indicates the huge demand for fresh organic produce.

The tokri scheme operates according to the growing seasons from November to January (winter), February to May (summer) and June to September (monsoon). Consumers pay a farm share of INR 3,000 in advance and in return receive a weekly mixed basket of seasonal vegetables for 16 weeks. Ubai Husein says that the price of subscriptions cannot really be compared to the conventional market, because MOFCA works with a cost-based model. The objective is for farmers to be able to recuperate the production cost and on top of that be able to earn a decent income for their labour. To that, only transport and packing costs are added as there are no profit-seeking intermediaries in the supply chain. Overhead costs are low because members of the consumer cooperative volunteer for administrative work and for part of the packing of the tokris. Initially, the tokris were packed in a private home in Bandra West, but in 2011, that work was shifted to a participating farm in Bhiwandi where hired helpers now work together with volunteers.

MOFCA takes its promise to supply farm-fresh vegetables seriously: Produce is delivered directly to consumers within 36 hours of harvest, without any storage. Wrapped in newspapers inside reusable plastic crates, the tokris travel by car to several pick-up points located in South Mumbai and the Western Suburbs. Members are requested to bring their own carry bags to the pick-up points. If consumers fail to pick up their tokris from the pick-up points, it is their loss because they have already prepaid for the entire season. Apart from a higher and more stable income, farmers benefit by not having to deal with middlemen or transport logistics, since produce is getting picked up directly from the farm.

The learning curve during the pilot phase was steep for the organizers, who are still in the process of refining the system and the supply chain. Due to limitations of supply, 250 kg of vegetables were delivered per week during the first growing season, which constituted only 50% of the initial target. By 2012-13, the target of 500-600 kg per week was reached. The initiative is successfully balancing the pressure of scaling up for financial viability with the objective of staying as local as possible. The quality, variety and consistency of supply of vegetables also improved significantly since the first season. The consumer members are receiving the model well, and especially those who take the opportunity of visiting the farms and participating in the grading and packing activities were seen to return with greater commitment to the project.

6 Conclusion

6.1 Summary of Findings

The overall objective of the present study was to examine the current state of the Indian domestic market for organic food in order to facilitate the growth and sustainable development of the market. Specifically, it aimed to identify and classify the systems of production, distribution and marketing that exist in three major urban markets of South and West India: Mumbai, Bangalore and Hyderabad. Another objective was to identify challenges in organic marketing, disseminate the lessons learned by various stakeholders and share best-practice examples of successful marketing initiatives. The study provides a reference for practitioners in the organic sector – such as producers, processors and retailers – and for policy makers.

Organic food sales and retail models

Among the three urban markets that this study analyzed, Bangalore is the largest both in terms of the number of stores that sell organic food products and in terms of organic sales. With an estimated INR 21.4 crore annual organic food sales, Bangalore is the largest urban organic market in India. By comparison, Mumbai has only INR 17.9 crore, and Hyderabad INR 9.9 crore of sales. These estimates are based on our count of outlets that stock organic products and an extrapolation from sales figures which were available from selected retailers. Bangalore also has by far the highest number of organic food outlets per inhabitant.

The distribution and retail models in urban markets were analyzed on the basis of a classification framework that takes into account a wide range of criteria in the areas of organizational structure, production and sourcing of organic products, product range, supply chain organization, marketing activities and consumer reach. We distinguished five major retail models, with several sub groupings each. The most important category in terms of organic food sales are organic specialty formats, which comprise organic specialty stores, non-food stores such as Fabindia, health food stores and markets.

Bangalore, as the largest market, had 23 organic specialty stores and 157 other stores of various formats that sold organic food in 2011. In Mumbai, the numbers are slightly smaller, with 19 organic specialty stores and 132 other stores. Hyderabad, the smallest organic market out of the three, had 6 organic specialty stores and 87 other stores in 2011. Other stores include non-food specialty stores, supermarkets and organized retail chains, general trade and miscellaneous small stores such as health food stores and cafés. While very few organic specialty stores were founded before 2005, there has been a wave of new shop openings since 2009. The greatest number of organic stores in all three cities opened between 2009 and 2011. In 2012, the growth continued at a similar or even accelerated rate.

Organic specialty stores were found to have a wide range of backgrounds, approaches and supply chain models. They are typically proprietor-owned, small stores with monthly sales volumes ranging from less than INR 1 lakh (for small stores and recent start-ups) up to INR 12 lakh (for larger and long-standing stores). The 16 stores in Bangalore from which we could obtain data reported average monthly sales of INR 2.5 lakh.

India has only a few organic specialty store chains, and no fully organic supermarket chains yet. One of the largest organic retail chains in India, Fabindia, was not counted as an organic specialty store, but rather as a non-food store because it deals mainly in textiles, furniture, and handicrafts. Natural food stores focus on products for healthy lifestyles, but – in contrast to organic specialty stores – organic products in these stores typically constitute less than half of the total product range. While Fabindia and organic store chains have India-wide, centralized supply chains, most organic specialty stores source both from local farmers, from smaller companies that operate on a sub-national level and from national-level branded processors. Products are a mix of certified organic branded products, non-certified products sourced regionally, and non-organic products marketed as "natural". Organic stores also increasingly brand their own products which they procure in bulk and package directly in the stores.

The most important sales channels are organic specialty formats, with organic specialty stores and non-food stores taken together. These are closely followed in total sales value by organized retail chains. Since 2009, most organized retail chains across India started adding branded and certified organic products to their range. Availability of organic food in supermarkets varies widely between different retail chains, between outlets of the same chain and between different parts of a city. While a few chains plan to sell organic products in all their outlets in the future, most of them focus on selected outlets in neighbourhoods with a high concentration of SEC A and B households. Typically, supermarkets source only from certified, national-level companies.

Sourcing from small farmers directly is not a viable option for organized retailers, because they require high volumes, quality and consistency of supplies. The exact number of supermarket outlets that stock organic products could not be determined in this study because sufficient information was not available from most retail chains.

In several cities, groups of urban consumers and farmers have started small-scale marketing initiatives that can be grouped under community-supported agriculture. The aim of these initiatives is to supply fresh, organically grown vegetables to consumers while building local networks of food supply between producers and consumers. They operate based on personal relationships, trust and transparent supply chains, rather than third-party certification. Supply chains are regionally oriented, with typically up to a few hundred members. Vegetable baskets are delivered to the homes of consumers or to pick-up points at various locations. Consumers become active members joining a cooperative, buying farm shares at the beginning of the season, or prepaying for their deliveries so as to give farmers more financial security and to share the risks of agricultural production.

While some of these initiatives supply a mixed basket of seasonally available produce, others allow consumer members to order individually every week. In both cases, close feedback loops to farmers and meticulous production planning ensure that supply matches the demand as closely as possible in order to minimize wastages. Community-supported agriculture encourages personal interactions between producers and consumers, for instance at farm visits. The objectives of the community-supported agriculture model is not only to supply sustainably grown vegetables, but also to support local organic farmers, to educate consumers about agricultural production and the seasonality of produce, to strengthen regional economic activity, and to reduce food miles by encouraging local and seasonal eating habits of urban consumers.

Since 2010, a growing number of online retailers and home delivery services started operations. Several e-commerce businesses focus on a natural lifestyle and sell organic food products as well as other product categories such as organic textiles, natural cosmetics and green home cleaners. A few conventional online retailers have also included organic products in their range. The product ranges of online retailers differ widely, and may include both certified and non-certified products, sourced from local, national and international suppliers. In some cases, online orders are merely an extension of an existing system of phone orders and home delivery. Regular organic retail stores increasingly include online order options into their service offering.

In the hospitality industry, a small number of restaurants, catering businesses and five-star hotels use organic ingredients. The highest number of restaurants is located in Bangalore, and several delivery services operate in Mumbai. While some of them have an explicit health orientation, others provide typical Indian restaurant food but made with organic ingredients. Most restaurants do not use exclusively organic ingredients because these are not consistently available, especially fresh vegetables.

Challenges in organic supply chains

Organic stakeholders, from producer groups to processors and retailers, face several challenges in managing supply chains successfully and sustainably. On the supply side, the main constraints are the limited number of organic producers and a lack of a wide product range. Also, most products are not available consistently around the year, especially fresh produce which has the highest demand from urban consumers of all product categories. For processors and retailers, one of the challenges is to source from scattered producers with no access to adequate transport and logistics infrastructure. Producers are also not well trained in quality control. This makes it difficult to ensure supplies of consistent quality and adequate quantity. Small and marginal producers, on the other hand, lack access to information and to markets which could enable them to reap an organic premium for their produce. Further, while chemical-based farming is massively subsidized, organic farmers do not have sufficient access to farm inputs, support for certification, training on organic production methods and adequate infrastructure for processing, storage and transport. Organic supply chains are often inefficient due to small volumes and long distances, bringing up transport costs disproportionately.

While some government support is available for organic production and certification, the institutional framework is not ideal for supporting small organic marketing organizations such as producer companies and community-supported agriculture initiatives. For instance, farmer producer organizations and social enterprises working in organic marketing lack access to capital through bank loans and other sources. Many of them opt for a hybrid model of organization, combining a commercial marketing company with non-profit NGO that enables them to access more sources of funding and loans, and to benefit from tax exemptions.

On the retail and consumer end, there is a lack of awareness of organic farming in general and of certification in particular. Consumers are not sure where organic products are available and how to verify whether a product is third-party certified, PGS certified, organically grown, or merely "natural". Various surveys conducted across India found that between 25% and 41% of respondents were willing to pay a premium for organic – provided product quality is high and organic standards are assured. Apart from certification, personal relationships with producers and marketers – for instance in direct marketing and community-supported agriculture initiatives – play an important role in building this confidence and in strengthening local sustainable food supply chains.

Many stakeholders are unable to meet customer needs in terms of product range, consistent availability and quality standards. A lack of reliability and professionalism often deters consumers who are generally inclined to try organic food. These points are closely linked to the supply constraints mentioned above. Generally, demand for organic products exceeds availability because supply volumes are insufficient and producers are unable to reach markets.

Successful models of organic food marketing

In order to address these manifold challenges, various stakeholders have developed a range of strategies that help them market organic products to urban consumers successfully. The central lessons that emerge from the case studies can be summarized as a combination of building a large and reliable producer base on the one hand, and managing supply chains efficiently and professionally on the other.

In order to build up a strong supply base, organic NGOs and marketing organizations have invested a lot in expanding the number of suppliers. Their activities include awareness raising among farmers, running demonstration farms, training in organic methods and quality control, facilitating farmer-to-farmer training programmes, assistance with production planning and certification support. Various systems of backward supply chain integration include tie-ups with producers, for instance in community-supported agriculture and producer-consumer cooperative associations, corporate farming and contract farming. While contract farming can solve the problem of unreliable supply for large organic processors and organized retailers, contract terms are often to the disadvantage of farmers.

Collectivisation is a key strategy for unorganized small and marginal producers. Farmer producer organizations such as cooperatives and producer companies allow small and marginal producers to pool their produce, access capital, increase their profit by owning their processing and storage facilities and improving their bargaining power vis-à-vis buyers. They also give farmers an opportunity to concentrate on farming as their core activity by hiring qualified professionals for other capacities such as accounting, public relations and marketing.

Commercial organic companies and organized retailers try to build consumer trust and loyalty with the help of brand development and either third-party certification or a company-internal quality assurance system. Farmer producer organizations mostly rely on PGS – sometimes in combination with third-party certification – and transparent supply chains for assuring consumers of organic production standards. Various marketing models work with short, transparent supply chains and close personal relationships with local farmers. This helps them to reduce transport costs, avoid margins for intermediaries, supply fresh produce efficiently, minimize losses and build consumer trust.

6.2   Recommendations

Based on our findings, we can make several recommendations for decision makers on the policy level, in the commercial organic sector and in the organic movement which can contribute to promoting the sustainable growth of the sector. At present, support for organic producers in the form of agricultural extension services, training and marketing assistance is delivered mainly by the NGO sector. However, if the domestic market for organic products is to be developed further and grow beyond its current niche status, policy changes in favour of organic agriculture are urgently needed. Agricultural support systems should be shifted from a focus on unsustainable chemical-based farming practices to supporting the development of alternative, sustainable farming systems.

While conventional farming receives preferential treatment in the form of subsidies for fertilizers, hybrid seeds, diesel and water, organic farmers are not supported for producing their own bio-fertilizers like compost and manure, and they are not rewarded for saving water and providing ecosystems services such as conservation of soils and biodiversity. Organic farmers also need more support for conversion to organic, training in organic farming methods and other extension services. Furthermore, there should be a shift of focus to research on organic agriculture in state universities and in ICAR institutes.

In the past, the focus of organic agriculture policies and support services was mainly on expanding organic production for export. Policies for organic marketing such as the development of NSOP and the India Organic label are targeted towards export, largely neglecting the specific requirements of the domestic sector. There is an urgent need to facilitate domestic market development and market access for organic producers, so that they can meet the growing demand by urban consumers. Currently, the main constraint for expanding organic sales in the domestic market are supply side issues like lack of a wide range of products, inconsistency in quantity and quality of produce, inefficient transport and lack of market linkages. Simultaneously, policies need to promote consumer awareness programmes in order to increase the popularity of organic food and the knowledge about production standards and labels.

While there are some government programmes to support organic production and certification, more activities are needed that facilitate market linkages. In some states, local governments are planning to support the creation of dedicated organic malls to provide retails space for small organic companies and entrepreneurs. On the policy level, the focus of government policies on organic should be shifted from export to the domestic market. For instance, the government could provide more active support for third-party certification as well as PGS. The third-party certification system in its current form is not feasible for most smallholder producers. A few companies and NGOs help producers to get organized for group certification and internal control systems. However, these are not free from problems, for instance in group certification processes, farmers may be highly dependent on the sponsoring company which owns the certificate (Singh 2009).

With the increasing importance of contract farming in organic supply chains, the legal framework has to protect the interests of farmers. While the current legislation provides a model contract, mechanisms need to be put in place to ensure that actual contracts give equal weight to farmer interests, and existing contract arrangements need to be monitored closely.

Lately, associations of organic stakeholders and businesses have come forward who do not look to the Government of India for financial support or funds for expanding organic production, but rather call for trade support and less export restrictions for organic products (Oneindia 2010). From the perspective of small and marginal farmers who constitute the bulk of producers in Indian agriculture, policy interventions are needed that make organic farming more viable and that improve their linkages with local and national markets.

Collectivisation of small and marginal farmers in farmer producer organizations such as cooperatives and producer companies is an important strategy that can facilitate conversion to organic production, value addition and market access. Current market asymmetries need to be addressed to enable smallholder producers to negotiate better with other market stakeholders. For instance, small farmers need better access to credit from banks and other sources of start-up and investment capital. Further, funds need to be made available for processing and storage units on the village level, and for suitable small-scale post-harvest technologies for processing and value addition. Infrastructure support could include the creation of common facility infrastructure for use by small start-ups, such as shared packing facilities, pre-cooling chambers, cold storage, refrigerated vans, non-chemical fumigation facilities and dedicated wagons in trains that do not use pesticides or fumigants. For producer organizations to become successful marketing initiatives, human resource development programmes are needed to train educated rural youth in professional management of farmer producer organizations.

As far as organic producers and companies are concerned, profession-alization of marketing activities and customer communication can help them to build a dedicated customer base. For instance, product supply and quality have to become more consistent in order to meet customer needs. Chakrabarti and Baisya (2009) recommend that retailers should understand how "affective commitment" is created among regular buyers, and tailor their marketing campaigns to these factors so that early adopters and occasional buyers can be converted into regular buyers.

Consumer awareness of the dangers of chemical farming and of organic agriculture as an alternative is slowly growing. In part, this is due to a recent increase in media coverage in newspapers and on television, and due to awareness raising campaigns of NGOs and organic companies. Nevertheless, additional efforts are required to educate consumers about the benefits of organic farming, and about certification and labels used in the domestic market. Trust in organic standards can only grow if consumers understand the principles of organic farming and the certification process better, which can happen through education campaigns as well as through direct contact with producers. No publicity campaigns were initiated by the government after introducing the NSOP and India Organic label. Campaigns could be used to spread awareness of both the India Organic and the PGS labels, and emphasize the differences between certified organic, in conversion and organically grown so that consumers can distinguish them from products marketed under labels such as "natural," "fresh," "green" or "pure".

Organic stakeholders should not focus on price as the most important selling point, but instead market organic as quality products that are worth paying a (reasonable) premium for. Consumers have to realize that the price differential between organic and non-organic food is partly an artificial one. It masks the subsidies for chemical farming, for instance the fertilizer subsidy, which in 2011 cost the Government of India INR 61,000 core. It also does not take into account the health costs of pesticide-related diseases nor the social cost of farmer suicides, and it does not account for environmental costs to soils, water, biodiversity and the climate. Furthermore, organic producers and processors receive little external support in the difficult start-up phase, and they do not benefit from large economies of scale which are inimical to the organic principle of operating in small and diverse closed-loop systems.

While many consumers and experts agree that higher prices for organic may be justified, prices would have to be reduced somewhat in order to reach a broader audience. Organic should not target only the SEC A and B segments, but aim to be inclusive both in terms of product price levels and in the style and language used to address target groups of various educational backgrounds. Rather than being perceived as a small, elitist niche of the food market, organic could thus become a building block in the transition to more sustainable food systems.

While keeping organic food prices affordable, farmers also need to be able to earn an adequate income. Many NGOs and producer companies have made fair trade principles an explicit part of their agenda and communicate the reasons for higher price levels to their customers in this vein. Commercial organic companies, however, do not necessarily have the farmers' benefit as their first priority while trying to place their brand in a competitive market. Price pressure has ruled the conventional food industry for a long time, and has led to a race to the bottom in terms of unsustainable farming practices, exploitative producer prices, declining food quality and corporatisation of production and retail. Such a trend is inimical to the principles of organic farming and sustainable development. The dilemma of keeping food prices affordable without compromising on fair and sustainable principles of production can only be achieved by giving greater support to sustainable production systems, rather than subsidizing harmful chemical-based farming system.

The example of price pressure versus sustainable practices shows that, as the organic sector in India grows and develops further, care has to be taken to avoid the "conventionalization trap" (El-Hage Scialabba 2005) that can be observed in developed organic markets. For instance, even though the strongest motivating factor for consumers in India who buy organic are health concerns (Naik and Sharma 1997; Chakrabarti and Baisya 2007; Osswald and Dittrich

2010; Dholakia and Shukul 2012), organic marketing should not focus only on health as the main selling point but frame organic food in a larger context of its contribution to sustainability. Marketing organic as healthy and cheap could easily lead to a sell-out on social and environmental values. Rather, consumers need a better understanding of these larger issues at stake. Consumers also need to understand that organic farming promotes food security and helps farmers earn a sustainable livelihood from farming. It is not only the consumers' health that is at stake, but larger issues of social and environmental sustainability which may come at a certain cost, but will be worth it in the long run for society as a whole.

Organic production is a huge opportunity for involving small and marginal farmers in agricultural value chains, improving the livelihood security of India's rural producers and contributing to the sustainable development of the country's agricultural sector, which consists of over 80% of small and marginal farms. Organic should be inclusive of small, local family farms rather than promoting only corporate and large farms, and it should actively promote the localization of supply chains. If support for these farms is neglected, the growth of demand for organic products in the country might benefit only large-scale, corporate organic agribusinesses rather than locally embedded, participatory food networks that serve society as a whole. Governments and local authorities can take an active role in creating an enabling environment for sustainable local food networks, for instance by providing spaces for organic farmers' markets free of cost.

Finally, we would like to point out that organic food is only one aspect of a holistic approach to healthy and sustainable food lifestyles. The choice of organic products is one of several building blocks of sustainable diets; others include choosing local and seasonal produce, reducing consumption of animal products and highly processed and packaged products, supporting smallholder producers, farmer collectives and fair trade mechanisms, and building strong local food networks (cf. Sustain 2002, 2010, and Osswald 2011). While these principles are implemented by community-supported agriculture initiatives on a small scale, they also need to be considered in policy decisions that shape the organic industry at large.

Appendix 1: Certification agencies accredited under NPOP

The following 24 certification agencies are accredited with one of the six accreditation bodies approved by Ministry of Commerce as per NPOP, namely Agricultural and Processed Food Exports Development Authority, Coffee Board, Spices Board, Tea Board, Coconut Development Board, and Directorate of Cocoa and Cashewnut.

No.	Name	Address	Certification Mark
1	Bureau Veritas Certification India Pvt. Ltd.	Mumbai (Maharashtra) www.in.bureauveritas.com	
2	ECOCERT Idia Pvt. Ltd.	Aurangabad (Mharashtra) www.ecocert.in	
3	IMO Control Pvt. Ltd.	Bangalore (Karnataka) www.imo.ch	
4	Indian Organic Certification Agency (INDOCERT)	Cochin (Kerala) www.indocert.org	

No.	Name	Address	Certification Mark
5	Lacon Quality Certification Pvt. Ltd.	Thiruvalla (Kerala) www.laconindia.com	
6	Natural Organic Certification Agro Pvt. Ltd.	Pune (Maharashtra) www.nocaindia.com	
7	OneCert Asia Agri Certification (P) Ltd.	Jaipur (Rajasthan) www.onecertasia.in	
8	SGS India Pvt. Ltd.	Gurgaon (Haryana) www.sgs.com	
9	Control Union Certifications	Navi Mumbai (Maharashtra) www.controlunion.com	
10	Uttarakhand State Organic Certification Agency (USOCA)	Dehradun (Uttarakhand) Email: ua_usoca@yahoo.co.in	
11	APOF Organic Certification Agency (AOCA)	Bangalore (Karnataka) www.aoca.in	
12	Rajasthan Organic Certification Agency (ROCA)	Jaipur (Rajasthan) Email: rocajpr.cb@gmail.com	

No.	Name	Address	Certification Mark
13	Vedic Organic Certification Agency	Hyderabad (Andhra Pradesh) Email: voca_org@yahoo.com	
14	ISCOP (Indian Society for Certification of Organic Products)	Coimbatore (Tamil Nadu) www.iscoporganiccertification.org	
15	Food Cert India Pvt. Ltd.	Hyderabad (Andhra Pradesh) www.foodcert.in	
16	Aditi Organic Certifications Pvt. Ltd.	Bangalore (Karnataka) www.aditicert.net	
17	Chhattisgarh Certification Society, India (CGCERT)	Raipur (Chhattisgarh) Email: cgcert@gmail.com	
18	Tamil Nadu Organic Certification Department (TNOCD)	Coimbatore (Tamil Nadu) www.tnocd.net	
19	Intertek India Pvt. Ltd.	New Delhi www.intertek.com	

No.	Name	Address	Certification Mark
20	TUV India Pvt. Ltd.	Mumbai (Maharashtra) www.tuvindia.co.in	
21	Madhya Pradesh State Organic Certification Agency	Bhopal (Madhya Pradesh) Email : md.mpsoca@gmail.com	
22	Biocert India Pvt. Ltd.	Indore (Madhya Pradesh) www.biocertindia.com	
23	Export Inspection Agency (EIA)	New Delhi www.eicindia.gov.in	
24	Odisha State Organic Certification Agency (OSOCA)	Bhubaneswar (Odisha) www.ossopca.org	

Appendix 2: Organic stakeholders by distribution channel and city

Category	MUMBAI		BANGALORE		HYDERABAD		TOTAL	
	Stake-holders	Outlets	Stake-holders	Outlets	Stake-holders	Outlets	Stake-holders	Outlets
Organic companies and brands [1]	9	3	17	8	7	2	**32**	**14**
Organic specialty stores [2]	15	19	22	23	6	6	**42**	**47**
Health food stores [3]	3	3	0	0	2	2	**5**	**5**
Non-food stores [4]	5	18	3	17	3	7	**12**	**43**
Organic/ natural bazaars [5]	0	n/a	1	n/a	1	n/a	**2**	**n/a**
Direct marketing [6]	2	1	1	1	4	2	**7**	**4**
Restaurants and catering [7]	9	3	7	7	5	11	**19**	**11**
Online retail and home delivery [8]	2	n/a	2	n/a	1	n/a	**4**	**n/a**
Traditional retail, other stores [9]	26	29	1	1	3	3	**29**	**33**
Organized retail [10]	11	76	16	123	9	60	**36**	**250**
Total number	**82**	**152**	**70**	**180**	**41**	**93**	--	--
Market coverage per 1 lakh inhabitants	**0.44**	**0.83**	**0.82**	**2.12**	**0.53**	**1.21**	--	--

Detailed explanations of distribution channels: see Chapter 4

(1) Companies with own production base and/ or own processing; including major branding and distribution enterprises, but excluding smaller retailer brands; counting only those that are headquartered in the respective city and not other companies who may also sell in those cities; also not counting companies that sell exclusively into export, and those that deal exclusively in organic cotton

(2) Stores with 50% or more of food range organic, including organic retail chains

(3) Stores with less than 50% of the food range organic, mostly small standalone outlets

(4) Standalone stores and chains such as Fabindia that focus on non-food products, for instance handloom garments and textiles, home decor, furnishings, natural cosmetics

(5) Commercial or non-profit markets that sell multiple organic brands

(6) Farmers' markets, farmer stalls and mobile stalls, community-supported agriculture, consumer cooperatives and non-profit marketing by NGOs on behalf of smallholder producers

(7) Restaurants, cafés, bistros, bakeries, catering and food delivery services that use partly or exclusively organic ingredients

(8) E-commerce or other retailers who sell exclusively through online or phone orders, excluding retail stores that offer an online order option

(9) Kirana stores and smaller specialty food stores

(10) Modern format supermarkets and hypermarkets, mostly organized chains and some standalone outlets

References

Ablett, Jonathan; Baijal, Aadarsh; Beinhocker, Eric; Bose, Anupam; Farell, Diana; Gersch, Ulrich; Greenber, Ezra; Gupta, Shishir and Gupta, Sumit (2007): *The 'Bird of Gold': The Rise of India's Consumer Market*. San Francisco: McKinsey Global Institute.

Adhavani, R. (2009): Women vow to fight against GM crops: Mobile bio-diversity festival concludes. *The Hindu*, February 14.

Altieri, Miguel A. (2009). Agroecology, Small Farms, and Food Sovereignty. *Monthly Review* July-August. Internet Source: http://agroeco.org/wp-content/uploads/2010/09/Altieri-agroecoMR.pdf [accessed January 8, 2013].

Alvares, Claude (2009): *The Organic Farming Sourcebook*. Mapusa: Other India Press and Third World Network.

Ananthasayanan; Kuruganti, Kavitha; Noronha, Neesha; Rammohan, Radhika and Lakshmi Kutty, Sreedevi (2013). *Small Organic Retail is Beautiful*. ASHA (Alliance for Sustainable and Holistic Agriculture). Internet Source: http://www.kisanswaraj.in/2013/02/18/small-organic-retail-is-beautiful-a-booklet/ [accessed February 25, 2012].

Ansari, Humaira (2010): Soon, a tokri of organic veggies at your doorstep. *DNA* August 26. Internet Source: http://www.dnaindia.com/speakup/report_soon-a-tokri-of-organic-veggies-at-your-doorstep_1428775-all [accessed May 16, 2011].

Anshu, Kumari and Mehta, Jitender (no year): *Promotion of Organic Food: Opportunities & Challenges*. National Institute of Agricultural Marketing. Internet Source: http://www.indiabschools.com/Promotion%20of%20Organic%20Foods.pdf [accessed January 15, 2009].

APEDA (2012): Organic Products. Internet Source: http://www.apeda.gov.in/apedawebsite/organic/Organic_Products.htm [accessed Au-gust 31, 2012].

Assocham (2010): Organized Retail Share Likely To Surpass 30% By 2013: ASSOCHAM. Press Release, June 24. Internet Source: http://www.assocham.org/prels/shownews-archive.php?id=2473 [accessed July 1, 2012].

Assocham (2011): Domestic organic sector to reach Rs 10k crore by 2015: ASSOCHAM. Press Release, July 10. Internet Source: http://www.assocham.org/prels/shownews.php?id=2974 [accessed July 22, 2011].

BDAI (2012): *Annual Report 2011-12*. Bio-Dynamic Association of India.

Bhattacharyya, P (2004): *Organic Food Production in India: Status, Strategy and Scope*. Jodhpur: Agrobios.

Bhosale, Jayashree (2011): Format of farmer producer companies sees resurgence Jayashree Bhosale, ET Bureau Oct 20, 2011. *Economic Times*, October 20.

Internet Source: http://articles.economictimes.indiatimes.com/2011-10-20/news/30301501_1_banana-growers-farmers-and-consumers-benefit-both-farmers [accessed October 15, 2012].

Blume, Georg (2012): In Indien boomt die Biobranche. *die tageszeitung*, February 16. Internet Source: http://www.taz.de/1/archiv/digitaz/artikel/?ressort=wu&dig=2012%2F02%2F16%2Fa0120&cHash=1bc7d297ee [accessed February 16, 2012].

Borah, Prabalika M. (2012): Back to the roots. *The Hindu*, June 28, Life & Style, Metroplus. Internet Source: http://www.thehindu.com/life-and-style/metroplus/article3580695.ece.

Businessworld (2011): The Old Kings... And The New. *Businessworld*, December 12, Trends: Retail and Consumer Goods. Internet Source: http://www.businessworld.in/en/storypage/-/bw/the-old-kings-and-the-new/365798.0/page/0 [accessed July 1, 2012].

Carroll, Arati Menon (2005): *India's Booming Organic Food Bazaar*. Internet Source: www.ia.rediff.com/money/2005/oct/17spec1.htm [accessed January 15, 2009].

Chakrabarti, Somnath (2010): Factors influencing organic food purchase in India: expert survey insights. *British Food Journal* 112 (8), 902-915.

Chakrabarti, Somnath and Baisya, Rajat K (2007): Purchase Motivations and Attitudes of Organic Food Buyers. *Decision* 34 (1), 2-22.

Chander, M. (1997): Organic Farming: Towards Sustainable Agricultural Development. *Social Action* 47 (1), 216–230.

Cole, C.V.; Duxbury, J.; Freney, J.; Heinemeyer, O.; Minami, K.; Mosier, A.; Paustian, K. et al. (1997): Global Estimates of Potential Mitigation of Greenhouse Gas Emissions by Agriculture. *Nutrient Cycling in Agroecosystems* 49, 221–228.

Coley, David; Howard, Mark and Winter, Michael (2009). Local food, food miles and carbon emissions: A comparison of farm shop and mass distribution approaches. *Food Policy* 34 (2), 150–155.

Datt, Deepti (2010): Tradition reborn at Mumbai's first organic Farmers' Market, March 25. Internet Source: http://www.cnngo.com/mumbai/shop/organic-farmers-market-bandra-680366 [accessed May 16, 2011].

Datta, Prosenjit (Ed.) (2010): *The Marketing Whitebook 2010-2011: One-stop Guide for Mar-keters*. New Delhi: Businessworld.

DDS (2008): *Farmer-Proofing Agricultural Research: Current Trends in India. A Fact Sheet*. Democratising Agriculture Series, Vol. 1. Hyderabad: Deccan Development Society.

Dharmadhikary, Shripad (2010): Chemical-Free Food: Organic Veggies in my Inbox. Internet Source: http://www.indiatogether.org [accessed June 18, 2010].

Dholakia, Jalpa and Shukul, Maneesha (2012): Organic Food: An Assessment of Knowledge of Homemakers and Influencing Reasons to Buy / Not to Buy. *Journal of Human Ecology* 37 (3), 221–227.

El-Hage Scialabba, Nadia (2005): Global Trends in Organic Agriculture Markets and Countries' Demand for FAO Assistance. Paper presented at the conference "Global Learning Opportunity – International Farming Systems Association's Round Table: Organic Agriculture". Rome: FAO.

European Bioplastics e.V. (2009): Position Paper July 2009: 'Oxo-Biodegradable' Plastics. Berlin: European Bioplastics e.V.

Eyhorn, Frank (2005): Success Story: Organic India. In: Willer, Helga and Yussefi, Minou (Eds.). *The World of Organic Agriculture: Statistics and Emerging Trends 2005.* Bonn and Frick (CH): International Federation of Organic Agriculture Movements (IFOAM) and Research Institute of Organic Agriculture (FiBL), 74-75.

Foodnavigator Asia (2012): India almost tripled organic exports last year, says government agency, May 29. Internet Source: http://www.foodnavigator-asia.com/Markets/India-almost-tripled-organic-exports-last-year-says-government-agency [accessed May 29, 2012].

Foodwatch (2008): *Organic: A Climate Saviour? The foodwatch report on the greenhouse effect of conventional and organic farming in Germany.* Based on the study 'The Impact of German Agriculture on the Climate' by the Institute for Ecological Economy Research (IÖW). Internet Source: http://www.foodwatch.de/foodwatch/content/e6380/e24459/e24474/foodwatch_report_on_the_greenhouse_effect_of_farming_08_2008_ger.pdf [accessed April 18, 2009].

Garibay, Salvador V. and Jyoti, Katke (2003): *Market Opportunities and Challenges for Indian Organic Products.* Internet Source: http://orgprints.org/00002684 [accessed January 15, 2009].

Government of India (2000): *National Agricultural Policy.* Department of Agriculture and Cooperation, Ministry of Agriculture. Internet Source: http://www.nls.ac.in/CEERA/ceerafeb04/html/documents/agri.htm [accessed August 5, 2009].

Government of India (2005): *National Programme for Organic Production.* 6th ed. New Delhi: Department of Commerce, Ministry of Commerce and Industry. Internet Source: http://www.apeda.com/organic/ORGANIC_CONTENTS/English_Organic_Sept05.pdf [accessed March 10, 2009].

Heinze, Karin (2012): India: Ambitious plans for developing the organic market, January 19. Internet Source: http://oneco.biofach.de/en/news/?focus=84217a7b-4d25-461d-bcd0-4e30b37b85d0&fromnewsletter=true.

Henderson, Elizabeth (2010): The World of Community Supported Agriculture. Keynote for Urgenci Kobe Conference 2010, 'Community Supported Foods and Farming' February 22, 2010. Internet Source: http://www.chelseagreen.com/content/elizabeth-henderson-the-world-of-community-supported-agriculture/print/ [accessed January 25, 2012].

Herrmann, Gerald A. (2010): Labelling, Branding, and Packaging of Organic Products: Critical Success Factors. In: Partap, Tej and Saeed, M. (Eds.). *Organic Agriculture and Agribusiness: Innovation and Fundamentals.* Tokyo: Asian Productivity Organisation, 115-124. Internet Source: http://www.apo-tokyo.org/00e-books/AG-22_OrganicAgriculture/AG-22_OrganicAgriculture.pdf [accessed May 31, 2010].

IBEF (2004): Tapping India's eco-farming potential. Indian Brand Equity Foundation. Internet Source: http://www.ibef.org/artdisplay.aspx?cat_id=86&art_id=4488 [accessed January 30, 2009].

IBEF (2008): Retail: Market & Opportunities. Indian Brand Equity Foundation. Internet Source: http://www.ibef.org/artdisplay.aspx?cat_id=28&art_id=19772 [accessed Janu-ary 30, 2009].

Images Group (2009): India Retail Report Summary. Internet Source: http://www.indiaretailing.com [accessed July 1, 2012].

Jishnu, Latha and Sood, Jyotika (2012): Organic Universe. *Down To Earth* July 16-31, 26–37. Internet Source: [accessed July 27, 2012].

Kalita, Anurag; Doshi, Kopal; Dalmia, Shristi; Baweja, Amit and Shetty, Ashit (2008): Fabindia. Study submitted to Dr. Raja Saxsena, School of Business Management NMIMS. Internet Source: http://www.scribd.com/doc/11569951/A-Marketing-Project-on-FabIndia [accessed May 8, 2009].

KICS and CWS (2012). *Assessing Social Enterprises: The Need for New Parameters.* Secunderabad: Knowledge In Civil Society and Centre for World Solidarity.

Kloppenburg, Jr.; Lezberg, Sharon; De Master, Kathryn; Stevenson, George and Hendrickson, John (2000): Tasting Food, Tasting Sustainability: Defining the Attributes of an Alter-native Food System with Competent, Ordinary People. *Human Organization* 59 (2) (July 1), 177–186. Internet Source: [accessed November 14, 2009].

Kneafsey, Moya; Holloway, Lewis; Venn, Laura; Dowler, Elizabeth; Cox, Rosie and Tuomainen, Helena (2008): *Reconnecting Consumers, Producers and Food: Exploring Alternatives.* Berg Publishers.

Von Koerber, Karl and Kretschmer, Juergen (2009): Ernährung und Klima: Nachhaltiger Konsum ist ein Beitrag zum Klimaschutz. In: Agrarbündnis e.V. (Ed.). *Landwirtschaft 2009: Der kritische Agrarbericht. Schwerpunkt: Landwirtschaft im Klimawandel.* Kassel, Hamm (Westfalen): ABL Bauernblatt Verlags-GmbH, 280-285. Internet Source: http://www.kritischer-agrarbericht.de [accessed November 17, 2009].

Von Koerber, Karl; Kretschmer, Jürgen; Prinz, S. and Dasch, E. (2009): Globale Nahrungssicherung für eine wachsende Weltbevölkerung: Flächenbedarf und Klimarelevanz sich wandelnder Ernährungsgewohnheiten. *Journal für Verbraucherschutz und Lebensmittelsicherheit* 4 (2), 174–189.

Kotschi, Johannes and Müller-Sämann, Karl (2004): *The Role of Organic Agriculture in Mitigating Climate Change: A Scoping Study.* Bonn: International Federation of Organic Agriculture Movements (IFOAM).

Kriesemer, S. Kathrin; Weinberger, Katinka and Chadha, M.L. (2009): Demand for and awareness of safely produced vegetables in India. *Research in Action* 5. The World Vegetable Centre.

Lass, Daniel; Bevis, Ashley; Stevenson, G.W.; Hendrickson, John and Ruhf, Kathy (2001): *Community Supported Agriculture Entering the 21st Century: Results from the 2001 National Survey.* Amherst, MA: University of Massachusetts. Internet Source: http://www.cias.wisc.edu/wp-content/uploads/2008/07/csa_survey_01.pdf [accessed February 10, 2012].

Lohr, Kerstin and Dittrich, Christoph (2007): *Changing Food Purchasing and Consumption Habits among Urban Middle-Classes in Hyderabad.* Research Reports for Analysis and Action for Sustainable Development of Hyderabad No. 3. Berlin: Humboldt-University. Internet Source: http://www.sustainable-hyderabad.in [accessed February 1, 2009].

McIntyre, Beverly D.; Herren, Hans R.; Wakhungu, Judi and Watson, Robert T. (Eds.) (2009). *Agriculture at a Crossroads: IAASTD Global Report.* Washington, D.C.: International Assessment of Agricultural Knowledge, Science and Technology for Development.

Menon, Manoj Kumar; Jagannath, S.; Roy, Jaydip and Khare, Sukanya (Eds.) (2009): *International Seminar: 'India Organic – Strategies to Surge Ahead'.* Bangalore: International Competence Centre for Organic Agriculture.

Menon, Manoj Kumar; Sema, Akali and Partap, Tej (2010): India Organic Pathway: Strategies and Experiences. In: Partap, Tej and Saeed, M. (Eds.). *Organic Agriculture and Agribusiness: Innovation and Fundamentals.* Tokyo: Asian Productivity Organisation, 75-86. Internet Source: http://www.apo-tokyo.org/00e-books/AG-22_OrganicAgriculture/AG-22_OrganicAgriculture.pdf [accessed May 31, 2010].

Misra, Savvy Soumya (2009): Made it. Cover Story: Agriculture. *Down to Earth* 16 (January 1-15), 31-38. Internet Source: [accessed April 18, 2009].

Murray, E.V. (no year): Producer Company Model – Current Status and Future Outlook: Opportunities for Bank Finance. College of Agricultural Banking. Internet Source: http://www.cab.org.in/Lists/Knowledge%20Bank/Attachments/2/Produce r%20Company%20Model.pdf [accessed October 15, 2012].

NAC Working Group (2013): Draft Recommendations of the Working Group on Enhancing Farm Income for Small Holders through Market Integration. National Advisory Council (NAC).

Naik, G. and Sharma, C.K. (1997): Domestic and International Market for Organic Food Products. Proceedings of 3rd IFOAM-Asia Scientific Conference and General Assembly on Food Security in Harmony with Nature, 1st-4th December, Bangalore, 359-363.

Niggli, Urs (2010): High sequestration, low emission, food secure farming – the potential of organic agriculture for climate change mitigation. Presentation at the IFOAM EU Group Organic Day in DG Environment, 20 April 2010.

Niggli, Urs and Fließbach, Andreas (2009): Gut fürs Klima? Ökologische und konventionelle Landwirtschaft im Vergleich. In: Agrarbündnis e.V. (Ed.). *Landwirtschaft 2009: Der kritische Agrarbericht. Schwerpunkt: Landwirtschaft im Klimawandel.* Kassel, Hamm (Westfalen): ABL Bauernblatt Verlags-GmbH, 103-109. Internet Source: http://www.kritischer-agrarbericht.de [accessed November 17, 2009].

Niggli, Urs; Fließbach, Andreas; Hepperly, P. and Scialabba, N. (2009): *Low Greenhouse Gas Agriculture: Mitigation and Adaptation Potential of Sustainable Farming Systems.* 2nd ed. Rome: Food and Agricultural Organisation (FAO). Internet Source:

ftp://ftp.fao.org/docrep/fao/010/ai781e/ai781e00.pdf [accessed May 12, 2010].

Niggli, Urs; Leifert, Carlo; Alföldi, Thomas; Lück, Lorna and Willer, Helga (2007): *Improving Sustainability in Organic and Low Input Food Production Systems.* Proceedings of the 3rd International Congress of the European Integrated Project Quality Low Input Food (QLIF). University of Hohenheim, Germany, March 20-23, 2007. Hohenheim: University of Hohenheim. Internet Source: http://orgprints.org/10417/ [accessed October 13, 2009].

Oneindia (2010): India's leading organic companies launch trade body. *Oneindia* December 14. Internet Source: http://news.oneindia.in/2010/12/14/indiasleading-organic-companies-launch-tradebody.html [accessed December 14, 2010].

Organicfacts (2006): Organic Food Consumption in India. Internet Source: http://www.organicfacts.net/organic-food/organic-food-trends/organic-food-consumption-in-india.html [accessed January 16, 2009].

Osswald, Nina (2011): How Green is Organic? In: Menon, Manoj K.; Roy, Jaydip; S., Bindu and N.K., Veena (Eds.): *Organics: Beyond Agriculture into New Vistas.* Proceedings of the International Seminar, BioFach India together with India Organic. Bangalore.

Osswald, Nina and Dittrich, Christoph (2009): *The Market for Organic Food in Hyderabad, India: Consumer Attitudes and Marketing Opportunities.* Research Reports for Analysis and Action for Sustainable Development of Hyderabad. Berlin: Humboldt-University.

Osswald, Nina and Dittrich, Christoph (2010): *Sustainable Food Consumption and Urban Lifestyles: The Case of Hyderabad/ India.* Emerging Megacities Discussion Papers 03/2010. Berlin: Europäischer Hochschulverlag.

OTA (2010): India Market and Regulatory Assessment: USDA Emerging Markets Program. Organic Trade Association. Internet Source: www.ota.com/pics/documents/MarketRegulatoryAssessment.pdf [accessed September 7, 2012].

Partap, Tej and Vaidya, C.S. (2009): *Organic Farmers Speak on Economics and Beyond: A Nation Wide Survey of Farmers' Experiences in India.* New Delhi: Westville Publishing House, International Competence Centre for Organic Agriculture and Centre for Organic Farming, Himachal Pradesh Agriculture University.

Pfeiffer, Ehrenfried E. (no year): Bio-dynamics: A Short Practical Introduction. Internet Source: http://www.bio-dynamics.in/BDintroEEP.htm [accessed July 1, 2012].

Polasa, Kalpagam; Sudershan, R.V.; Subba Rao, G.M.; Vishnu Vardhana Rao, M.; Rao, Pratima and Sivakumar, B. (2006): *KABP Study on Food and Drug Safety in India: A Report.* Hyderabad: Food & Drug Toxicology Research Centre, National Institute of Nutrition.

Prabu, M.J. (2009): A farmer develops an herbal pest repellent after suffering from chemical pesticides: The farmer suffered a severe paralytic stroke for nearly three years. *The Hindu* February 26.

Prasad, Y.G. (2008): Bio-Intensive Integrated Pest Management in Organic Farming. In: Venkateswarlu, B.; Balloli, S.S. and Ramakrishna, Y.S.

(Eds.). *Organic Farming in Rainfed Agriculture: Opportunities and Constraints*. Hyderabad: Central Research Institute for Dryland Agriculture, 96-101.

Pretty, J.N. (1995): *Regenerating Agriculture: Policies and Practice for Sustainability and Self-Reliance*. London: Earthscan.

Radhika, P.; Ammani, P. and Seema (2012): Eating Healthy: Consumer Perception of Organic Foods in Twin Cities. *International Journal of Marketing, Financial Services and Management Research* 1 (2), 67–72. Internet Source: [accessed March 23, 2012].

Raidu, D.V. and Ramanjaneyulu, Gangula Venkata (2008): Community Managed Sustainable Agriculture. In: Venkateswarlu, B.; Balloli, S.S. and Ramakrishna, Y.S. (Eds.). *Organic Farming in Rainfed Agriculture: Opportunities and Constraints*. Hyderabad: Central Research Institute for Dryland Agriculture, 179-185.

Ramanjaneyulu, Gangula Venkata and Chennamaneni, Ramesh (2007): *Pesticides, Residues and Regulation: A Case Study of Vegetables in Hyderabad Market*. Research Reports for Analysis and Action for Sustainable Development of Hyderabad No. 10. Berlin: Humboldt-University.

Ramanjaneyulu, Gangula Venkata and Rao, Vijay Rukmini (2008): Sustaining Agriculture-Based Livelihoods: Experiences with Non-Pesticidal Management in Andhra Pradesh. *Development* 51 (4), 1-7.

Rao, C.H. Srinivas; Venkateswarlu, V.; Surender, T.; Eddleston, Michael and Buckley, Nick A. (2005): Pesticide Poisoning in South India: Opportunities for Prevention and Improved Medical Management. *Tropical Medicine and International Health* 10 (6), 581-588.

Rao, Kishore (2006): *PGS A Market Perspective: Perceptions to Organic Foods and Certification/ Labels/ PGS Concept in India*. New Delhi: Food and Agricultural Organisation (FAO).

Rao, Kishore; Supe, Raj; Menon, Manoj Kumar and Partap, Tej (2006): *The Market for Organic Foods in India: Consumer Perceptions and Market Potential. Findings of a Nation Wide Survey*. Bangalore: International Competence Centre for Organic Agriculture.

Reachout Hyderabad (2008): SPAR launches its 1st Supermarket in Hyderabad. Internet Source: http://www.reachouthyderabad.com/business/bizretail/spar.htm [accessed March 18, 2009].

Research and Markets (2011): Indian Organic Food Market Analysis. Internet Source: http://finance.yahoo.com/news/research-markets-indian-organic-food-155100228.html [accessed August 1, 2012].

Richter, Toralf and Kovacs, Annamaria (2005): Strategies to support domestic organic markets in countries with emerging organic sectors. Paper presented at the conference Researching Sustainable Systems – International Scientific Conference on Organic Agriculture, Adelaide, Australia, September 21-23, 2005. Internet Source: http://orgprints.org/4455/ [accessed May 8, 2009].

Roy, Devesh; Birol, Ekin; Deffner, Katharina and Karandikar, Bhushana (2010): Developing Country Consumers' Demand for Food Safety and Quality: Is Mumbai Ready for Cer-tified and Organic Fruits? In: Bennett, Jeff and

Birol, Ekin (Eds.). *Choice Experiments in Developing Countries: Implementation, Challenges and Policy Implications.* Chel-tenham/Northampton, MA: Edward Elgar Publishing, 261-277.

Scialabba, Nadia (2010): Sustainability and Organic Agriculture. In: Menon, Manoj Kumar; Roy, Jaydip and Chandra, Anushi (Eds.). *International Seminar: Improving Access to Global Organic Markets.* Bombay Exhibition Centre, Goregaon, Mumbai, 8-9 December 2010. Bangalore: International Competence Centre for Organic Agriculture, 25-27.

Seyfang, Gill (2006). Ecological citizenship and sustainable consumption: examining local organic food networks. *Journal of Rural Studies* 22 (4), 383-395.

Seyfang, Gill (2009): *The New Economics of Sustainable Consumption: Seeds of Change.* Palgrave.

Sharma, Subodh; Bhattacharya, Sumana and Garg, Amit (2006). Greenhouse gas emissions from India: A perspective. *Current Science* 90 (3), 326–333.

Singh, Jagdish (2004): Organic Farming and Agribusiness for Food Security in India. In: Singh, Tapeshwar (Ed.). *Resource Conservation and Food Security: An Indian Experience Vol. I.* Concept Publishing, 277-288.

Singh, Radhika (2011): *The Fabric of Our Lives: The Story of Fabindia.* Penguin Global, October 5.

Singh, Sukhpal (2009): *Organic Produce Supply Chains in India: Organisation and Governance.* Ahmedabad: Allied.

Singh, Tapeshwar (Ed.) (2004): *Resource Conservation and Food Security: An Indian Experience Vol. I.* Concept Publishing.

Sinha, Sukesh Narayan; Rao, M. Vishnu Vardhana and Vasudev, K. (2012): Distribution of pesticides in different commonly used vegetables from Hyderabad, India. *Food Research International* 45 (1) (January), 161-169.

Soil Association (2009): *A Share in the Harvest: An action manual for community supported agriculture.* 2nd ed. Internet Source: http://www.soilassociation.org/LinkClick.aspx?fileticket=gi5uOJ9swiI%3d&tabid=204 [accessed January 15, 2012].

Srivastava, Roli (2009): Supermarkets shut shop, face rent crisis. *The Times of India,* February 5.

Sudershan, R.V.; Subba Rao, G.M.; Rao, Pratima; Vardhana, M. Vishnu and Polasa, Kalpagam (2008a): Knowledge and practices of food safety regulators in Southern India. Nutrition & Food Science 38, 110–120.

Sudershan, R.V.; Subba Rao, G.M.; Rao, Pratima; Vardhana, M. Vishnu and Polasa, Kalpa-gam (2008b): Food safety related perceptions and practices of mothers: A case study in Hyderabad, India. *Food Control* 19 (5), 506–513.

Surendran, Sunilkumar (2010): Organic Food Retailing in India. In: Menon, Manoj Kumar; Roy, Jaydip and Chandra, Anushi (Eds.). *International Seminar: Improving Access to Global Organic Markets.* Bombay Exhibition Centre, Goregaon, Mumbai, 8-9 December 2010. Bangalore: International Competence Centre for Organic Agriculture, 106-113.

Sustain (2002). *Local Food: Benefits, Obstacles and Opportunities.* Sustainable Food Chains Briefing Paper 1. London: Sustain.

Sustain (2010). 7 principles of sustainable food. Internet Source: http://www.sustainweb.org/sustainablefood/ [accessed May 20, 2010].

Thakur, D.S. and Sharma, K.D. (2005): Organic farming for sustainable agriculture and meeting the challenges of food security in the 21st century. *Indian Journal of Agricultural Marketing* 60 (2), 205-219.

The Nielsen Company (2007): Unavailability and price the major reasons for Indians not purchasing organic products. Internet Source: http://in.nielsen.com/news/20071203.shtml [accessed January 16, 2009].

UNEP/ UNCTAD (2008): *Organic Agriculture and Food Security in Africa.* United Nations. New York and Geneva: UNEP-UNCTAD Capacity-building Task Force on Trade, Environment and Development. Internet Source: http://www.unctad.org/en/docs/ditcted200715_en.pdf [accessed May 1, 2010].

Wackernagel, Mathis and Rees, William E. (1996): *Our Ecological Footprint: Reducing Human Impact on the Earth.* Gabriola Island: New Society Publishers.

Wiggerthale, Marita (2009): *Zur Kasse bitte. Die neue Konsumfreudigkeit und boomende Märkte in Indien: Welche Folgen es haben kann, wenn Supermarktketten nach Liberalisierung des Einzelhandels rasch expandieren.* Berlin: Oxfam. Internet Source: www.oxfam.de/download/zur_kasse_bitte.pdf [accessed December 11, 2009].

Willer, Helga and Kilcher, Lukas (Eds.) (2012): *The World of Organic Agriculture – Statistics and Emerging Trends 2012.* Frick and Bonn: Research Institute of Organic Agriculture (FiBL) and International Federation of Organic Agriculture Movements (IFOAM).

Yadav, A.K. (2009): Organic Agriculture Going Mainstream in India. In: Menon, Manoj Kumar; Jagannath, S.; Roy, Jaydip and Khare, Sukanya (Eds.). *International Seminar: 'India Organic – Strategies to Surge Ahead'.* Bangalore: International Competence Centre for Organic Agriculture, 2-4.

Ziesemer, Jodi (2007). *Energy Use in Organic Food Systems.* Rome: Food and Agricultural Organisation (FAO). Internet Source: http://www.fao.org/docs/eims/upload/233069/energy-use-oa.pdf [accessed October 23, 2009].

www.ingramcontent.com/pod-product-compliance
Lightning Source LLC
Chambersburg PA
CBHW032003190326
41520CB00007B/343